C000178727

WOOD CARVING

PROJECTS AND TECHNIQUES

GUILD OF
MASTER CRAFTSMAN
PUBLICATIONS

WOOD CARVING

PROJECTS AND TECHNIQUES

CHRIS PYE

First published 2007 by
Guild of Master Craftsman Publications Ltd

Castle Place, 166 High Street,
Lewes, East Sussex BN7 1XU

To Dan & Shona

Text and photographs © Chris Pye
© in the Work GMC Publications 2007

ISBN: 978-1-86108-507-8

All rights reserved

The right of Chris Pye to be identified as the author of this work has been
asserted in accordance with the Copyright Designs and Patents Act 1988,
sections 77 and 78.

No part of this publication may be reproduced, stored in a retrieval system or
transmitted in any form or by any means without the prior permission of the
publisher and copyright owner.

This book is sold subject to the condition that all designs are copyright and
are not for commercial reproduction without the permission of the designer
and copyright owner.

The publishers and author can accept no legal responsibility for any
consequences arising from the application of information, advice or
instructions given in this publication.

A catalogue record for this book is available from the British Library.

Illustrations on pages 33, 73 and 75 by Simon Rodway
Author photo on page 171 by Susan E Lowry

Managing Editor Gerrie Purcell
Production Manager Jim Bulley
Editor Virginia Brehaut
Managing Art Editor Gilda Pacitti
Designer James Hollywell

Set in Bembo

Colour origination by AltaImage
Printed and bound in by Sino Publishing

Contents

Introduction

I wrote my very first article about carving for the first ever issue of *Woodcarving* magazine. I have continued to write pretty regularly for the magazine ever since, giving much time and effort to crafting and presenting projects that I thought would be of interest to readers.

As the months and years rolled by, the stack of past issues on my bookshelf – representing a huge block of words – grew layer by layer. I came to think of my articles as being squashed like strata, destined never to be found without some hefty shovelling. Some I managed to extract and re-shape into my book, *Elements of Woodcarving.* The rest I thought lost... perhaps forever.

But thankfully, as *Woodcarving* edges nearer to its one hundredth issue, my publishers have ventured to undertake an archaeological dig. As a result, some of the better bones have been resurrected, re-mounted, and, indeed, preserved in the very book you now hold in your hands.

I am extremely pleased not to have lost this material. Here you have a mix of techniques and practical projects that have arisen from specific commissions or simply good old-fashioned bright ideas. Some of the projects are very straightforward and easily reproduced; others are much more involved and serve as a guided tour of the process of carving.

I have been through the articles carefully and with few exceptions have not felt the need to make changes. I hope you find much that is interesting and useful, perhaps even an odd little gem, as you work your own way through this archaeological dig.

I would like to thank GMC Publications for allowing me to write for them over the years and for the opportunity to re-present these articles. In particular, I have benefited from, and deeply appreciate, Virginia Brehaut's assembling of this book so conscientiously, and my good friend Mark Kimble's deft ability with words.

Chris Pye
2006

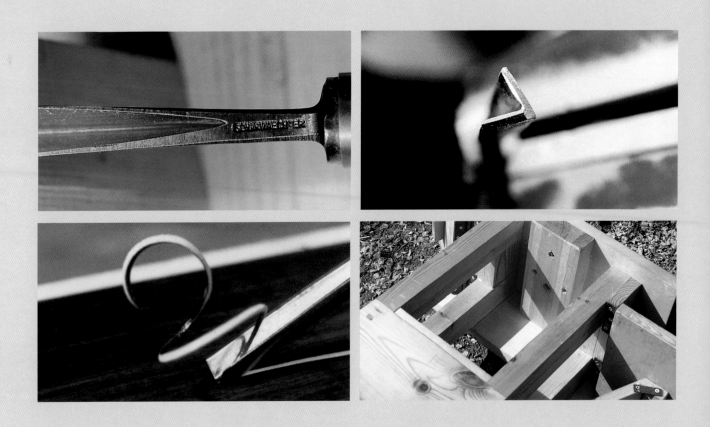

Part One
Tools and Equipment

- **Selecting and Sharpening a V Tool**

- **Holding and Using a V Tool**

- **Bench Work**

◄ A collection of V tools in various angles, sizes and profiles.

Selecting and Sharpening a V Tool

The V tool has a reputation for being tricky to use and sharpen. This step-by-step guide to selecting and sharpening will help carvers get to grips with this versatile tool.

The V tool is one of the most useful tools to the carver. There is always at least one V tool on my bench and it is a rare carving where I do not use one somewhere. Unfortunately, the helpful V tool has a reputation for being difficult to sharpen and tricky to use. I have known newcomers to give up completely and banish it to a neglected corner.

I hope to de-mystify V tool sharpening and to show some of its potential as a carving tool. Carvers are served by many well-established, specialist carving tool makers, but poor tools can escape quality control. To avoid potential difficulties here is a checklist of what to look for when buying one, then a step-by-step guide on how to sharpen a V tool and keep it sharp. So if you are having difficulties with the V tool, start here. I hope you find it more friendly and useful and less a tool to approach with trepidation.

There are three angles of V tool available. The most acute angle is 45° and gives a deeper, narrower cut. The widest angle is 90° which gives a broad, shallow cut. I recommend the middle 60° angle as most useful for the newcomer. Buy a straight one, No 39 in the Sheffield List (see page 162). The width of a V tool is measured from corner to corner in a straight line, and a full range of widths is available from most carving tool manufacturers. A good size to begin with is ⅝in (16mm). Like other carving tools, V tools are available straight, shortbent (spoon) or longbent (curved) profiles, the latter two for working in hollows.

▲ Opposite above left: Finely made shoulder and shank but the alignment of the cannel (the inner hollow) is out of true. Although not so evident with the end of the full blade length, as the tool becomes shorter so this fault will become more evident.

▲ Opposite below left: Bellying on the inside means it cannot be sharpened with a flat stone on the outer bevel without removing a notch of metal near the apex. The inner walls should be flat.

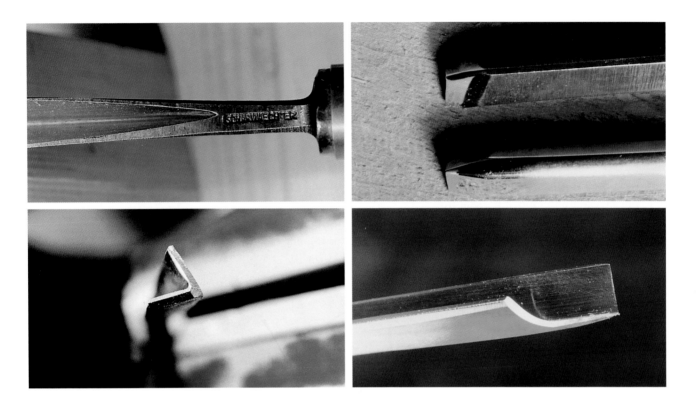

As your carving progresses you will find both smaller and larger sizes useful, in different angles and bends, ending up with a small range. Sharpening and use of the different angles of tools is similar. I will be using the straight 60° x ⅝in (16mm) tool as my model.

Choosing a V tool

Here is a checklist for choosing a good V tool:

1   Good steel, well tempered. If you buy from a reputable manufacturer you can assume this. Beware of cheap tools from market stalls.
2   Polished or black outside finish is a matter of personal preference only and has no functional significance.
3   Straight axial line to the blade and tang, with the blade fitted straight to the handle.
4   Walls of equal thickness, relatively thin, with the inside V groove aligned along the axis of the tool giving a uniform appearance to the blade along the length.
5   Inner wall faces should be dead flat with no bellying. Look at the tool end on. Bellying is a bad fault and makes the tool more difficult to sharpen. You can correct the fault with a slipstone, but I would reject such a tool.
6   Keel about the same, or only a little more than the thickness of the walls. There is necessarily more metal at the keel where the two walls of the V tool join.

▲ Top right: A keel with a correct amount of metal and below, one which is very thick.

▲ Centre right: If the keel is too thin, as here, the pressure from the wedge effect of the outside bevels can be disastrous, snapping the metal at the junction when the tool is used vigorously.

▲ Above: Where there is a lot of metal in the junction the keel can be ground back to make less of a wedge to push into the wood.

The keel

The keel is not a sharp edge but slightly rounded, allowing it to negotiate corners smoothly. As a rule, the less metal here the better for the carver, which is why thin walls are preferable. The keel is where manufacturers encounter most problems in forging (such as the metal cracking) and some play safe by making the junction a thicker mass. The result is the keel is a large wedge or cone of metal needing more force to push it through the wood and always tending to rise out of the cut. And fine lines with the V tool are virtually impossible. You can and should correct this fault by carefully removing metal from either side of the keel where the heels of the side bevels meet it. This at least helps lessen the force needed to push the tool along. Besides the obvious keen cutting edge which gives a very clean, polished cut, you should be aiming for the features of the V tool shown in the drawing below.

The parts and features of a correctly sharpened V tool.

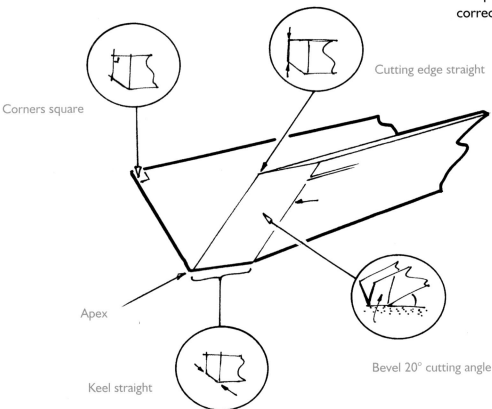

Corners square

Cutting edge straight

Apex

Bevel 20° cutting angle

Keel straight

Manufacturers sometimes nose the apex or wing the corners. This has more to do with the way the tool is made than with the needs of carvers. Unless you have a particular application for a nosed or winged tool, square and straight is the most useful shape. The keel and bevel angles are the same, around 20°, a little more for harder woods and a little less for softer ones. The bevel angle translates into the cutting angle, that at which the tool starts cutting the wood. This gets higher if bevel or keel is rounded. It is important to keep the bevels flat and the keel straight.

Sharpening

Equipment

You will need the following equipment for sharpening:

1 Bench grinder for initial shaping and setting the bevel. Remember to keep the blade cool by frequent water dipping.

2 Coarse carborundum benchstone for refining or replacing work done on the grinder. Some beginners find the grinder stressful. It removes metal too fast for their comfort and they end up overgrinding and misshaping the V tool. If you feel like this, use the coarse benchstone wherever I have indicated the grinder. You can achieve exactly the same effect, only it takes a little longer.

3 Fine, translucent, Arkansas benchstone, used with light oil for producing the final keen edge.

4 Fine, translucent, Arkansas angle-edged slipstone used with light oil for cleaning off the wire formed by the benchstone. The slipstones must fit exactly into the inner angle, otherwise it is easy to notch the edge.

5 Benchstrop and slipstrop dressed with a fine abrasive like crocus powder and tallow for polishing up the final cutting edge and maintaining its sharpness.

The sharpening process

Work methodically and in a relaxed way, reading through everything first to make sure you understand the process. Exactly how much grinding, if any, you need will depend on the state of the tool. Check what effect you are having on the blade by looking frequently at the white line of light along the cutting edge. The secret is to keep this even at all times. If one part of the bevel thins, showing as a thinning of the line, then carefully work on the thicker part of the bevel and return the white line to a uniform thickness before proceeding with the whole bevel. Also look at the scratch marks on the bevel. These will show clearly how you are offering the bevel to the grinder or benchstone.

Correcting the 'conical keel' fault by removing excess metal on either side.

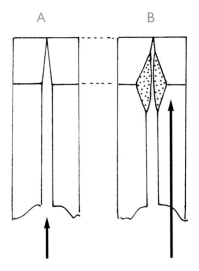

A

V tool with too thick a junction, as the two sides meet.

B

Grind off thick corners here between keel and heel to ease the tool through the wood. Leave keel at correct cutting angle.

Square the edge

Hold the V tool perpendicular to the grinder, that is pointing to the wheel axle. If the tool was originally nosed, or the walls thicker towards the apex, the edges will now look, end on, wedge-shaped. (See step 1 on flow chart overleaf.)

Polish the edge

A few perpendicular passes on the Arkansas benchstone or equivalent ceramic stone to flatten, clean and refine the metal which will be the final cutting edge. Check the white line for a polished surface all across. (See step 2 on flow chart overleaf.)

Set the keel angle

Present the keel across the grinding wheel at an angle of about 20°. Imagine the surface of the wheel is the wood you will eventually cut and present the keel at the angle you would like to be cutting. The thickness of the white line at the apex will reduce and begin to look cut off. Aim to end with a metal thickness of about 1mm at the apex. (See step 3 on flow chart overleaf.)

Set the bevel angles

Use the grinder to begin with and finish with a light touch to the side of the wheel or the flat coarse benchstone. The V tool is essentially two chisels joined at one side to form an angle, and this is the best way to regard it. Concentrate on the 'chisel' you are working on and ignore the other for now. The bevel angles should be the same as the keel, 20°, rendering the white lines the same thickness as at the apex and looking even. The apex will still look cut off. It will get special treatment later. (See step 4 on flow chart overleaf.)

Sharpen the bevels

Make sure the bevels are flat. Whether the edge is parallel to the heel will depend on whether the walls are of equal and even thickness. The keel will almost certainly be longer than the bevels. This is fine as long as it is straight and at the correct cutting angle. Use the carborundum to thin the white line to about 0.5mm, or go straight to the Arkansas or ceramic benchstone if the edge is less from accurate grinding. The benchstones should be end on to you. Treat each side of the V tool like a chisel and reduce the line evenly. Take great care to keep the bevels flat. Check the white line and bevel scratches to make decisions as to exactly how the tool should present to the stone. If the line thins at any point, slightly turn the wrist to exert a little more pressure on the thicker part of the edge and away from the thinner part. Occasionally take off the wire edge with the slipstone and push the edge into some medium hard wood to toughen it up.

Continue until the white line attenuates and disappears on both sides. You will be left with a point of light at the unsharpened apex, probably projecting a little with a hook which must now be sharpened separately. Finally soften the heels with a few specific strokes on the Arkansas stone. (See step 5 on flow chart overleaf.)

Sharpen the apex

Turn the Arkansas stone side-on and lay the keel flat on the surface. Rock the tool from side to side, and carefully hone the keel until the spot of light at the apex, with the hook, disappears. Use the slipstone to clean the wire edge from the inside of the angle. Overworking the keel will dip the apex back. Finally, soften the heels where the bevels meet the rest of the blade, including the junction where the keel meets the heel, with a few passes on the Arkansas stone. (See step 6 on flow chart overleaf.)

Test the edge

Try the tool on some close-grained wood such as lime (*Tilia vulgaris*). It should leave polished cuts, close together, with the root of the cut being clean, without snail tracks or scratch marks. It is crucial the cutting apex and edges of the V tool, the parts which leave the finished cut, are properly sharp, otherwise a ragged cut is inevitable. Tiny spots of light and scratch marks can be touched up with the slipstone.

If the V tool ends up with the edge dipping at the apex, wavy, or in other ways unsuccessfully sharpened, one or two perpendicular strokes of the Arkansas benchstone will straighten and clean the edge back and reveal the white light from which to start again.

Stropping

Finally, strop the outside on the benchstrop and inside with the slipstrop. Carefully wipe the blade and the tool should sing along as it cuts the wood. If you strop the tool regularly the edge will remain sharp. After a lot of stropping the bevels will tend to round over, but a quick honing to flatten them will return the tool to an efficient state. (See step 7 on flow chart.) If your tool is bought sharpened you can select what you need to do to improve the overall performance or restore sharpness.

The process of sharpening a V tool

Step	Action	Equipment	
1	**Square edge**	Grinder or coarse benchstone.	
2	**Polish edge**	Fine, translucent Arkansas benchstone.	
3	**Set keel**	Grinder etc.	
4	**Set bevels**	Grinder etc. Setting the bevel angles. Start with this orientation to the wheel (left) which will produce a slight hollowing of the bevels. Finish flat bevels on the side of the wheel (right).	
5	**Sharpen sides (wings)**	Fine, translucent Arkansas etc. Plus slipstone.	
6	**Sharpen apex**	Fine, translucent Arkansas etc. Plus slipstone.	
7	**Strop**	Bench and slipstrops.	

Squaring off the end of the V tool on the grinder.

End view showing thinner walls towards the corners and the coarse striations in the metal caused by the grinder. As this metal contains the final cutting edge, it needs to be polished.

Polish the end on the fine benchstone, pulling the blade vertically towards yourself.

End view now showing a polished surface ready for shaping the keel and bevels.

Setting the keel angle on the grinder.

End view. Setting the keel causes the apex to look cut off. A small thickness of metal should still be left.

To remove the hollow, finish off the bevel using the flat side of the wheel. Grinding wheels are not designed to take sideways pressure, so only the lightest touch should be applied.
End view. After grinding, the white line has been reduced to a uniform thickness. Ignore the cut-off look to the apex for now.

From shaping on the grinder, move to sharpening on the fine benchstone, treating the two sides like chisels. Keep the bevels flat and at a consistent angle, thinning the white line equally on either side.
End view. The white line has practically gone on the sides but is still present at the apex.

Finish off the apex by rubbing the keel on the fine benchstone.

Removing the burr on the inside with a slipstone.

A benchstrop will polish up and put a final keen edge to the V tool.

Strop the inside with an appropriately shaped slipstrop.

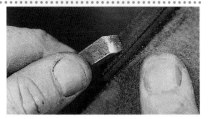

Holding and Using a V Tool

Holding and using a V tool is a skill that needs to be practised in order to learn tool control. These practical exercises will help to perfect the technique.

In this country a less common name for the V tool is parting tool. Old carving books sometimes called it a dividing tool. The name used in France, burin, points to the V tool's other main use: engraving (literally digging into) or decorating a surface in a shallow sketch-like manner.

To learn the best way to hold and manipulate a V tool you will need a piece of flat wood to practice on and a keenly sharpened V tool. Fold your left hand around the blade so as to cover the ferrule and a little of the handle, with your thumb on the handle. Grip the tool lightly but firmly and rest the heel of this hand on the workpiece. Hold the handle comfortably with the right hand or back hand. This is the principle grip for cutting to the left. But because the tool presents to the surface of the wood at a low angle it is important to be able to swap hands and use the V tool from both directions. This avoids body contortions or having to turn work around. So reverse hands for cutting to the right.

▲ Above left: The correct way of holding a V tool when cutting to the left.

▲ Above right: It helps if you can reverse hands for cutting in the opposite direction.

Basic principles

Here are some basic principles for cutting with a V tool:

The front hand must always rest on a surface, usually the workpiece but if necessary the bench or clamp. The only exception is if you are using a mallet. The back hand propels the tool forward. The front hand acts as a brake, limiting the forward push. This means there is always some tension between the two hands and you must feel this. You should be able to start and stop the cut at will.

Control of direction comes mainly from the wrist of the front hand, pivoting on the little bone that rests on the wood, sliding along as necessary. Fingers also play a role, as do the arms and body. In general keep your elbows in and support the cutting with your body. You will find your body swings around as the cut curves.

You can set a constant cutting angle with the front hand. The groove you create will be of even depth and width. Lowering and raising the handle will produce shallower (narrower) or deeper (wider) grooves. Keep the tool corners clear of the wood to prevent tearing up the grain. To make a deeper groove either repeat the stroke or use a larger V tool.

Practice

Make some smooth and flowing lines, including parallel cuts along the wood with the V tool, bearing in mind these principles. You will see how difficult it is to make cuts in opposite directions without swapping hands, so do practise changing over.

Try some deeper cuts, still keeping the corners clear but this time tilting the tool to the left or to the right. You will now have three different profiles of cut, relative to the wood surface, for different jobs: symmetrical, or with a more upright wall to the left or to the right. This is seen in practice in project 2, on page 24.

Now start a slow, curving cut which winds tighter and tighter to form a helix in the centre, swapping hands as necessary, and you will observe the following point: as one side of the V tool cuts with the grain, the other cuts against it. In other words, there can be a good and a bad face to the cut with the grain clean or torn. This is less of a problem with denser wood and sharp tools, and both sides of the cut will be clean when running across the grain.

Always try to direct your cut so the clean face is against your subject, and any tearing to the waste, say the background of a relief. If there is no waste side, as in the projects later, you my need to run the cut in the opposite direction, slightly tilted, to clean up the rough face.

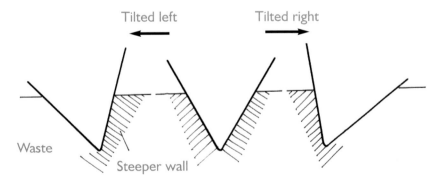

Tilting the V tool to one side produces a very useful cut, seen in project 2, in which an edge can be formed at the same time as some of the waste is removed.

Curves

The V tool judders and snatches the grain as the curve gets tighter. This happens because the sides (or wings) of the V tool are behaving like chisels, which they are, as a tool negotiates a bend. The deeper the groove the sooner the outside wall of the cut is crushed by the heel.

In carving we can overcome this problem in various ways, for example using bent tools, or coming in from above with a gouge. So V tools are really only suitable for slow curves when used to any depth. If you use the apex only can you get a shallow cut round a tighter bend. In either case the bend is limited and you will have to resort to gouges to finish off curves. The root or bottom of the V trench is rounded. It needs to be, as a sharp keel and internal angle would tend to force the tool like a jig in a straight line, against the direction the carver wishes. Small cuts using just the apex are almost identical with those made with a veiner, a small deep gouge. In many cases the veiner is the better, more convenient tool.

Parting

In both relief carving and in the round, the V tool is used to run a groove which separates one part of a carving from another. In low relief carving where the separation is from the waste wood, such as the background, this is known as lining and is a preliminary stage to setting in.

To line in a design you work quickly and closely around a subject, outlining it with the V tool, bearing in mind the need to put rough sides of the cut to the waste. The surrounding wood is then removed and gouges chosen to set in curves and details of the design to give a precise shape. Lining in presents damage to the design during the wasting process and prevents the crushing of fibres and consequent crushing of weak parts, which may happen if gouges are thumped straight into the wood.

Tool control practice

In the following projects I use the V Tool somewhat like an engraving tool to draw out my design. I create three effects by treating the background differently each time. The design I am using comes from *The Book of the Kells*, a drawing of a Celtic hunting dog. I chose the design for its simple shape and flowing curves which give the best effects. I used Jelutong (*Dyera costula*) for the carving, but any light-coloured light-density wood such as lime (*Tilia vulgaris*) will do. Start with a clean planed surface. In each case I could press through the paper onto the wood and leave enough of an impression to follow, with the help of a good cross light. No cleaning up of pen lines was necessary. You'll need a skew chisel and a few gouges for the tight curves and surface modelling.

▲ The V tool is separating the subject from its surroundings…

▲ …which are then reduced. The subject itself may need setting in more accurately with other carving tools.

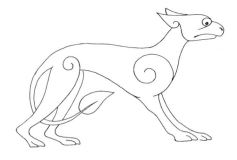

▲ This drawing, supposedly a hunting dog, is taken from *The Book of Kells*. Many Celtic designs look well treated in the manner of these projects.

Project 1

This line-only sort of carving is a real test of tool control. I have seen plates and vases engraved like this in the Black Forest, where the carvers use palm tools **1**.

I first coated the light wood with about 3 layers of dark varnish to form a surface skin. Do not use a penetrating stain. Impress the drawing onto the dried varnish. You will see I added a box of lines in the background to visually fix the dog **2**.

Grooves will show up white as you carve through the varnish. You must try to carve each line right first time. Try to relax. Go for good, flowing lines and avoid flats **3**. Start with the longest lines and bring others in to join them, varying line width for interest **4**.

Nick ends off with the skew, never tear them **5**. As mentioned, a small veiner will also tackle this work just as well. The V grooves of tight, small curves are best done with gouges **6**. It is not necessary to slavishly follow the drawing. Better to cut fresh, more spontaneous inaccurate lines than rather accurate ones badly. There is no reason why you should not sketch freehand in this manner.

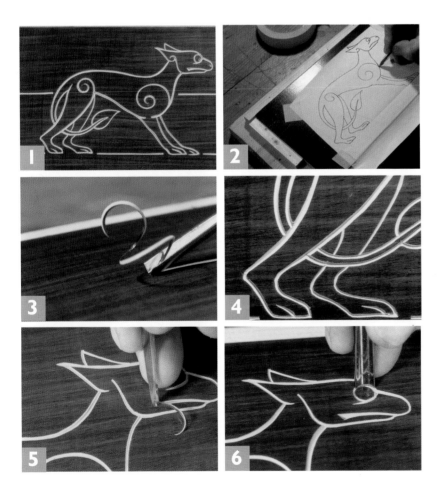

1 The Celtic hunting dog, engraved into light wood through layers of varnish.

2 Pressing through the paper onto the wood leaves an impression which can be followed.

3 The first long sweeping stroke with the V tool.

4 A close-up of the engraving effect of the V tool.

5 Where lines do not run into other lines the ends must be nicked off with a skew chisel.

6 Curves which are too tight for the V tool, such as the eye, will need to be cut with appropriate carving tools.

Project 2

Cavo-relievo, literally hollow relief, is the technical term given to a style of carving, perfected by the Egyptians, where the background is not cut away. Rather the subject appears sunk into it. Most of the subject remains at original surface level **7 8**.

Impress the design on the wood and incise the design as with the last project. This time make a point of tilting the V tool into the design so the outlining wall is more vertical and the design itself has a more bevelled look to its edge. When all the defining grooves are finished you can turn to modelling the subject.

Round over the bevelled edges with the skew chisel, merging with the main surface of the dog. You may need to repeat or touch up the original V lines. Legs and other elements can be separated out and modelling put in as with any relief carving, but keep the work simple and flat **9**.

The principal body surface is best finished with a flat gouge. This is a quick way of working compared with having to remove the background. Also the design itself is protected within the outlining walls **10**. These may be some of the reasons why cavo-relievo was adopted as a technique by the Egyptians.

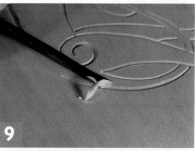

7 The dog treated cavo-rilievo, where the surrounding wood is the original surface.

8 Close-up of the face.

9 After the lining in with the V tool, round over the form with a skew chisel.

10 The broad surface is slightly finished with a flat gouge.

Project 3

Frosting or matting is when a background is worked over with fine-toothed punches . Frosters or frosting tools can be made in different sizes or shapes from a small triangular file from large nails or bolts. The froster can be applied to the background either randomly, or in patterns, or a mixture of both which is what I will describe here.

Normally the background is left with the plain texture, but in this case I have added colour. Incise the dog with the V tool as in the first project, but this time to a uniform depth . Also add a framing line. Start the frosting by working around the dog carefully. Place the edge of the froster in the root of the V groove crunching down the outer wall of the V and leaving a clean wall against the subject only .

For the rest of the ground, hold the froster a little above the surface so when thumping down into the wood it springs back like a piston. Work systematically over the whole ground and you will see the dog standing out strongly . I coloured the whole surface with a bright blue water-based dye and when dry lightly rubbed back the main surface of the dog with fine sandpaper. The frosted background will appear a lot darker because of the bruised end grain.

Next I wiped a non-tarnishing gilt wax available from art shops across the frosted surface, taking care not to obliterate the blue stippling. The blue should show through gold . The wax dries and then the whole piece can be buffed to a polish.

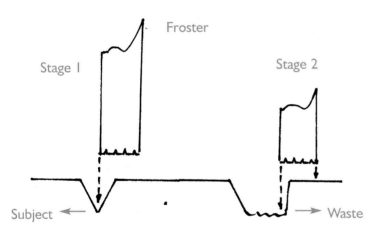

Define and protect the edge of the subject before working the froster more into the background.

Summary

These three simple projects show just a few of the interesting effects the V tool can help to create when it acts as an engraving tool. There are many more and I hope this chapter stimulates you to discover them.

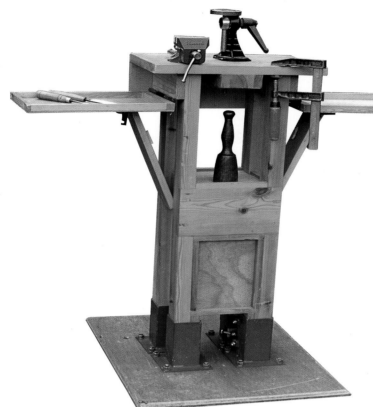

◄ The carving bench in all its glory.

Bench Work

This home-made carvers' bench is portable and inexpensive to make. Why not build your own with spare oddments and fittings following the features described here?

Portable benches have a logistics problem – they need to be light enough for you to carry them from A to B but at the same time strong and stable so they can be used to carve on. They need to be high enough for you to stand comfortably, without being too wide or heavy. If they are too small there will be nowhere to put your tools – too large and you will have to pack a gorilla to help you move it. My solution was to make a portable bench using those inexpensive metal post holders found at garden centres, typically used for assembling fences or gazebos on, say, a concrete patio.

I started by bolting four metal post holders to a baseboard on which I would stand. The legs of the bench insert into the metal 'box' and are fixed by tightening the side bolts firmly. Thus, I provide the necessary weight by means of what I carry around with me anyway.

I made the bench up – quite literally from the bottom up – with little planning. So, in this chapter, it will be best if I describe the features of the bench – ie how it 'works' – but give you only a few measurements, so you can adjust elements such as height to whatever suits you best. I used wood oddments and fittings lying around the workshop so, other than the post holders, the bench costs very little.

Features of the bench

It is a workstand that disassembles easily and is light and small enough to fit in the back of my car, yet strong and stable enough for me to carve at it standing up.

You can clamp small relief panels to the good overhang of the top.

There is a flat vertical work surface on the 'back'. Besides strengthening the structure and giving me a place to hang my name, this board gives me another way of clamping flattish work.

I can lay out my mallet and gouges on the two foldable and detachable side trays.

My tool rolls sit on the small shelf beneath midway down.

I keep important items safe in the lockable cupboard.

The baseboard

I started by bolting the post holders to a wide plywood board. Underneath this baseboard, I glued an old rubber car mat for grip and protection against the damp of the ground should I be outdoors. Note how close the brackets are together. This is because I wanted the narrowest possible arrangement – after all the bench does have to go in the back of my car.

When the legs of the bench are inserted into the brackets they are locked solid, like a column, and the working height can be that of my normal bench. I stand on the board and it's all too well weighted.

▲ Above: The bench set-up ready for carving.

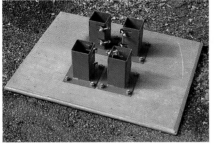

◀ Far left: The baseboard with the four post holders.

◀ Left: The bench legs lock into post holders.

The frame

I added the legs to the post holders and then the crosspieces to make the basic bench frame. To this I added the top and trays. There are two sets of crosspieces – at the top and halfway down. The traditional arrangement is four crosspieces between the four legs but I purposely missed out two at the top to gain clearance for clamps and spanners.

The vertical and top work surfaces themselves, screwed to either crosspiece, provide the missing strength. Two main lower crosspieces are wider and housed into the legs at right angles to the top ones. The remaining two crosspieces at this level are simply screwed from the inside. The post holders add the missing strength here.

Once you have the frame assembled, add the top and front panel. Make cupboards and shelves by nailing battens within the frame and covering with plywood.

▲ Housing joints at the top – crosspieces thick enough to screw the top to. A centre-strengthening block is included for work-holder fixing bolts that pass through the top.

Side trays

The trays are held in position by an arm which folds down into the space between two side legs. When extended, the end of an arm butts up against a block glued to the underside of the tray. Lastly, the trays themselves can be removed. I used hinges that separate into two parts.

Summary

I hope you can see how you might adapt some of the ideas in this very useful portable bench. The bench easily comes apart into small units for transport and is quick and simple to assemble. It is strong because it locks to the holders in the baseboard and your own weight keeps it stable. It won't take big stuff of course, but enough for demonstration purposes of round and relief carving. The tool trays are very convenient for organizing your carving.

There's also the issue of space. Many carvers I have spoke to complain that they haven't room for a bench. This excuse doesn't work if you make this bench as it can easily fit in a cupboard in someone's house.

▲ Above left: Tray and brace. I found it easy to bump the arm off the block and spill the tools, so a metal plate locks the arm to the tray.

▲ Above: Once folded down, a little toggle on the arm keeps it in place while travelling.

Construction

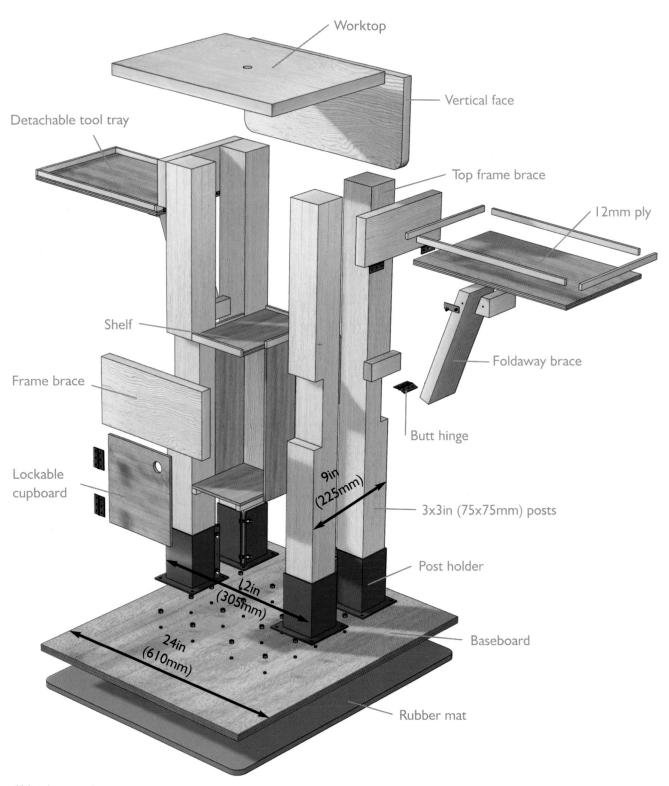

Worktop

Detachable tool tray

Vertical face

Top frame brace

12mm ply

Shelf

Foldaway brace

Frame brace

Butt hinge

Lockable cupboard

9in (225mm)

3x3in (75x75mm) posts

Post holder

12in (305mm)

24in (610mm)

Baseboard

Rubber mat

*Height to suit user
*All dimensions for assembled construction

Part Two
Architectural Carving

- **Learning Curve**

- **Pineapple Finial**

- **Lion Brackets**

◀ The finished scroll and handrail.

Learning Curve

This classic exercise in shaping uses careful handwork and some machinery to carve an attractive handrail scroll for a stairway.

There are many ways of dissuading young children from sliding down staircase handrails, the presence of a knob on the bottom newel post being the most common. Personally I find a horizontal turn or scroll at the bottom of some handrails a more elegant solution – flinging the slithering child to either left or right.

It just so happens that I recently had to make such a scroll to end the handrail on a newly built and very elegant staircase. While joiners can be considered experts on straight lines, curves are often out of their territory, particularly three-dimensional ones. It is here that we wood carvers can step in and help. Making this turn or scroll was a classic exercise in shaping – using some machines (the bandsaw and router) but still relying on careful handwork (gouges, spokeshave, rasps and sandpaper). There is also a logical process and sequence of steps which makes carving the scroll a relatively straightforward exercise.

Design

The scroll itself is a continuation of the handrail, so I made sure I had a section (profile) from which to work. The 'button' or disc into which the scroll turns is a little thicker than the handrail itself. It looks nicer, is less plain, and adds emphasis to the end of the handrail. This extra thickness means that as the handrail completes its downward run in a curve and turns to the side, it rises up again slightly as it disappears into the scroll. Before I began drawing out I needed some important reference points (see facing page). I was able to obtain all these measurements from the staircase plans.

Important measurements for the handrail scroll

(A) The angle at which the stair (handrail) would rise – remember the scroll lies truly horizontal.

(B) The point where the handrail starts to rise – part of the work was to carve the smooth curve whereby the handrail turned into the horizontal scroll.

(C) The centre point of the scroll – this sits above the centre point of the bottom ('curtail' or 'scroll') step, where it projects to the side and beneath the scroll.

(D) The distance between the centre point of the scroll and the handrail.

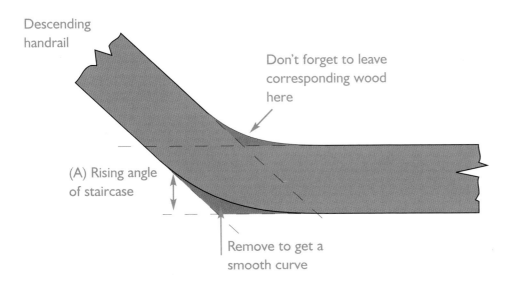

Descending handrail

Don't forget to leave corresponding wood here

(A) Rising angle of staircase

Remove to get a smooth curve

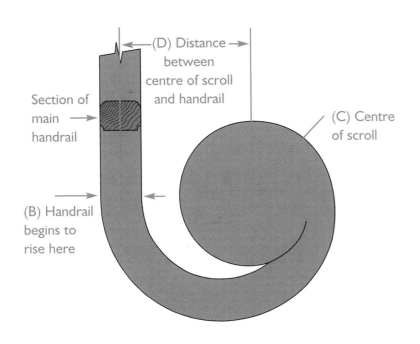

(D) Distance between centre of scroll and handrail

Section of main handrail

(C) Centre of scroll

(B) Handrail begins to rise here

Sketching out

Once these reference points had been marked on a large piece of paper, I started drawing out the scroll freehand . I drew with a 2B pencil on paper with a 'tooth' aiming for long, flowing lines. A trick here is to start with several light, 'gesture' lines before firming up your final one.

I am often asked why I don't use a computer for this sort of drawing. I could, but there are several reasons why I choose not to. I haven't a programme, or more importantly the time to learn one, and I can draw a smooth curve already reasonably quickly. I also get the important 'feel' for a scroll through my hand as I draw. Last but not least I enjoy drawing, so why give up something I derive pleasure from doing anyway? From my drawing, I made an accurate template of the handrail profile from plastic. I was certain to need this if I was to be accurate once I left the straight and narrow .

Wood and cutting out

The handrail and scroll were both in oak (*Quercus spp.*) and I always begin with neatly planed timber. The grain of the scroll orientates parallel with the handrail, which I decided to make in two parts. This would help in cleaning up the inside of the scroll more easily and also enable me to bandsaw the handrail section as it rises up and away from the rest of the scroll.

The working drawing was transferred from paper to wood via carbon paper and the bandsaw was used to cut the scroll and handrail section . I turned the handrail section on its side and cut the curve that heads it up the stairs.

I allowed a margin of ⅛in (3mm) outside the lines in case there was untoward flex in the bandsaw blade as it went round these tight curves. Smooth, continuous and accurate sawing minimizes mess, saving valuable time when cleaning up. I keep all the waste pieces as they make perfect packing blocks or 'formers' when the two parts are glued together later.

Squaring off

I shaped both the scroll and rising sections accurately square, using a spokeshave for the outside convex surfaces and a fine rasp for the inside convex surfaces **4** and **5**. I left what will be the join of two parts only roughly formed. This is a very important stage as the square profile is a 'witness' – the logical underlying form of the scroll as it turns and unravels into the handrail. Once you get this right, all subsequent shaping of the profile will look right too.

1 Drawing out the curves by eye. My hand, in the picture, naturally wants to pivot at the wrist and draw a curved line – you can use this anatomical feature to guide smooth and true curves.

2 The handrail template cut out of hard, thin plastic.

3 The two parts of the scroll after bandsawing. The rail part on the right must be turned on its side and the rising curve re-sawn. The disc or button part on the left will be thicker to the rail that sweeps into it.

Routing

With the workpiece still in two parts, I decide to rout the cove on the underside . Obviously I needed a cutter that matches the cove. If you don't have a router you will have to handcarve with an appropriate gouge. The easiest way of holding the scroll was with double-sided sticky tape although hot-melt glue would do the trick.

The cutter won't actually fit the inside sharp corner of the scroll, where the handrail meets it, so this has to be carved by hand . I started with the centre V tool cut and finished off either side of the cove with a deepish gouge.

Gluing up the two parts

Now the two parts could be glued together. With parallel grain there is no need to dowel or strengthen the joint by any other means. I used sash clamps and 'formers' – cradle-like blocks from the bandsawn offcuts – at each end to help grip the wood . Without these formers the curved shapes would just slip out of the clamps as I applied pressure. I simply tacked the waste blocks to the scroll parts with hot-melt glue. The blocks easily came away when I had finished but, should they have proved difficult, I could have always warmed the hot glue up with a hair dryer.

Shaping

I cleaned up underneath the scroll on a flat board with sanding paper after the glue had set. I also checked the position and accuracy of the rising angle. I then turned to both the inside and outside of the curves, shaping and cleaning across the join and making absolutely sure everything was still square.

Turning the scroll over, I completed routing the cove as far as I could into the handrail. I finished the remainder with a deepish gouge . I had drawn a profile of the handrail on this end of the rising part and worked towards this. At this stage, a third (perhaps a half) of the profile of the scroll carving was finished – the lower side, the flat sides and the small flat on the top, the last two the result of squaring the wood neatly.

The trick in cutting the handrail into the disc part of the scroll is to run the form as a square section first. It may seem like extra work but you do progress much more accurately. The disc is thicker than the handrail so I drew a slowly rising line towards the disc or button as a guide and cut away wood with a flat gouge **10**.

I started the shaping on the outside curve, using the template as my guide and making pencil lines to help me. I used a variety of tools such as spokeshaves, rasps, files and inverted flat gouges to keep the lines smooth and flowing. You cannot measure this so you must trust your eye **11**.

4 Squaring the outside of the scroll with a spokeshave.

5 Cleaning and squaring the inside of the scroll with a fine rasp.

6 With the disc held up with double-sided tape, I routed the cove at the edges.

7 Finishing off the cove junction of the handrail disc.

I carefully checked the width of the handrail and carved the inside face around the half-crescent space. I carved around the button with a V tool to finish. I smoothed the surfaces as well as I could using my hand tools and finished off with ever finer grits of sandpaper, dampening the wood in between grades **12**.

8 Gluing together the two parts. Note how the handrail section has been bandsawn from two directions.

9 Finishing off the underside of the handrail as it emerges from the disc. The angle of rise here is crucial.

10 The handrail rises up into the thicker disc, narrowing and losing the inner face as it winds in.

11 Shaping the profile of the handrail and disc – the template is a great help in ensuring consistent uniformity.

12 Final sanding. Note the section of the handrail hot-melt glued to the end of the rising part. When it is eventually fitted the joiner must neatly merge the handrail properly with the scroll.

Summary

I would say the most important aspects of this project were keeping the square profile as long as possible, and so sneaking up on the final form, and using my eye to seek the truest lines and curves.

◄ Completed Brazilian Mahogany finial; height 8in (200mm).

Pineapple Finial

This fine finial displays the popular and enduring pineapple motif. The aim here is to show how a relatively simple carving of an accurately laid-out design can give an impressive result.

A finial typically finishes off the top of a bedpost or pediment, usually pointing up. Terminating ornaments that point down are normally called 'drops'. Finials can be turned, carved or a mixture of both. Traditional motifs are urns, flames, eagles, but with fruit, only the pineapple has ever been popular. The tropical pineapple has historically been an exotic delicacy, reserved for the wealthy and sophisticated who are exactly the clientele who commissioned furniture and carving. The pineapple also lends itself to stylization and simplification, while retaining a lot of interesting shapes and shadows.

I was asked to make a finial similar to an existing gilded one, but with radically simpler leaves. This example uses only two tools for the pineapple itself and a few others for the leaves: V tool, flat gouge of chisel, medium sweep gouges and skew chisel. I used a salvaged offcut of South American mahogany. This takes good detail and leaves a smooth, tight surface for the gilding. Of course you may have to match the wood to the furniture or job in hand. French polishing suits them very well.

1 Turning the finial on the lathe. Only the non-carved parts are sanded, to protect the carving tools from embedded grit.

2 The lengthways lines have been marked and those of the circumference are now being calculated.

Turning the blank

The advantages of turning an initial blank finial are numerous, even if you don't need the lower turned bead and hollow elements. You can consider the turning as the initial 'bosting in' stages of the carving. The more accurate the pre-carved blank, the more accurate the marking out and the eventual tidiness of the final carving – making them easier to duplicate.

With an indexing plate you can mark lengthways lines quickly. The lathe can be used to hold the finial while you are carving it. Without a plate you will have to adapt something to hold the carving between ends; or grip the finial by its spigot. The 'between centres' turning is simple. At the drive centre end I left a spigot for fitting **1**.

At the tailstock end I came as close as I dared to the final tip or point of the finial, visualizing where this point would end within the remaining nub of waste wood. I actually came a little too close, and made the end too weak to take the subsequent side forces of the carving. Luckily I had a small jubilee clip with which to strengthen the waste nub.

Everything that was to be left uncarved I sanded to a finish. I left the pineapple and leaf surfaces as smooth as possible from the skew (turning) chisel. Essentially the pineapple effect is the result of two overlapping barley-sugar twists spiralling in opposite directions. Both twists are marked out. The first is cut, then the second, overlaying the first.

Marking out

The ridges (bines) of barley twists between the hollows are normally rounded and soft. However, by keeping the ridges sharp, the overlapping, opposite spirals result in lozenge-shaped pyramids which characterize the stylized pineapple. Pineapple finials always look better if the pyramids become smaller as they approach the point. For this you will need to lay out your spirals carefully, so the pitch of the barley twists decrease towards the point, shortening the length in which the twist returns to the starting line. You can mark out the pineapple by eye, simply by wrapping spirals of masking tape around the blank. It's worth doing this to get a rough idea of the position of the spiral line.

The grid

The real advantage of a grid drawn on the wood comes when you want to reproduce your finial accurately. Mark the lengthways lines by dividing the circumference into 16 parts with an indexing plate **2**. This gives the right proportion of squares to start with, but you can have more and smaller squares by making more divisions.

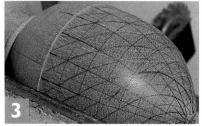

3 These lines represent the troughs of what in effect are overlapping barley-sugar twists.

4 Marking out completed for one direction of spiral. Note how the circumferential lines close up towards the tip. The two colours make sure I distinguish ridges from troughs and do not cut wood where I shouldn't.

5 Using a V tool to cut a groove along the line of the troughs.

Lacking an indexing plate, a simple method is to wrap a strip of paper around the circumference at its widest point. Fold and crease the strip in half, and then fold each half again to give quarters. Repeat the folding until the strip is divided into 16. Transfer the divisions back to the finial. Mark out lines around the circumference to produce squares. Use dividers to mark out a first square, using the width of one of the lengthways divisions at the leaves for the length. Mark the following circumference lines at decreasing increments, according to the decreasing width between the lengthways lines as they progress towards the finial point. In this way you end up with squares on the pineapple surface, getting smaller to the point of the finial. Draw the spirals **3**. Join up the diagonals of the squares to produce spiral lines. As you cut the twists you are effectively turning the squares at 45° so giving them their lozenge-like appearance. Important: you have both ridges and troughs in a barley twist. You need to draw two spirals – one representing where wood is left, the other where it is removed.

Accuracy

The result of your drawing so far is designed to give you accurate lines to begin carving and produce a lovely pineapple. Aim to continue this accuracy – I strongly advise you run these lines in different colours **4** to make sure you leave wood in the right places. Lock the carving firmly. A common mistake is cutting the angled troughs of the component barley-sugar twists – and thus the pyramids – too deep. They can be fairly shallow (as here) and still produce a strong effect. Carve the ridges in one direction first. Start with a V tool and run a channel along all the lines designated as troughs, all in one direction **5**. Cut just shallower than your final depth, and cut each groove the same. Use a mallet if the wood is hard. The very point of the finial must be finished off later; for now, groove as far along to the end as possible.

Carving the ridges

Use a flat gouge or chisel and cut one side of the ridge **6**, working with the grain. Do this as neatly as you can, leaving a flat face from the bottom of the trough (cut by the V tool) to the line designated to be a ridge, which is left visible. Reverse direction and carve the other side of the ridge **7**. The result will be sharp-edged twists in one direction, getting tighter towards the point. Re-mark the lines, twisting in the opposite direction, drawing the lines down and up the sides of the ridges. Repeat the process, starting with the V tool, following the diagonal line from corner to corner **8**. Cut the sides of these second ridges with the grain, as before **9**. The result should be a set of spiralling pyramids.

6 Working with the grain, I cut the face of one side of the ridge with a flat gouge.

7 Now reverse direction, to keep with the grain as I cut the opposite side. A chisel can also be used.

8 Re-mark the opposite spiral lines and begin again with the V tool.

9 As before, cut the sides of the ridges with a flat gouge or chisel; now the pyramids start to appear.

The leaves

Inevitably they will need some truing and cleaning up. Again, cut cleanly and not too deep. You can run the V tool along the troughs for a softer effect. In this pineapple there are four big primary leaves, and four smaller secondary ones, in between. Use the indexing plate (or paper strip method) to mark divisions and draw out your leaves carefully **10**. If you are not happy doing this by eye, make a paper or card template. Start by lining in (outlining) the main leaves with the V tool **11**. Line in the smaller leaves. Use a skew chisel to shape the lower pyramids into the waste spaces between bigger and smaller leaves.

Detailing the leaves

Set in the outline of the leaves with a matching sweep of the gouge **12**. Shape the leaves with medium gouges. I simply hollowed the sides to leave a central vein effect along the mid-lines. 'Draw in' the veins by sweeping in curving lines towards the middle with the V tool **13**. However you shape or carve them, the leaves must look as if they envelop the pineapple: don't make the mistake of carving the leaves too small, so that the pineapple looks as if it would never fit. For finishing the point, the finial must come off the lathe. Grip the spigot in a vice and saw off the waste wood – but not too much. Visualize the tip to where the spirals will run. Check and draw your lines. Run the V grooves smoothly round to end at the point. Carve the decreasingly smaller ridges by eye with the flat gouge or chisel, until they disappear at the point.

Finishing

Check your work, clean up any rogue pyramid facets or lines. Lightly wipe the pyramid with fine (240 grit) sandpaper, as the carving will probably have quite sharp corners. These pyramids feel a lot pleasanter if the sharp edges are (very lightly) softened, though over-sanding will kill the crispness that marks out a well-made pineapple.

10 Primary and secondary leaves being marked out.

11 Here I outline a leaf with the V tool.

12 Shape the pyramids into the waste with a skew chisel – it's a tight angle to get into.

13 Simple V grooves give the appearance of veins.

◄ The completed pair of
brackets: near-identical twins.

Lion Brackets

This stunning pair of brackets with lion's head
pediments were a challenging commission designed
to sit on the plinth of a door frame.

The two brackets, each with its lion's head, volute and foliage, are
replacements for a similar pair that were fixed either side of the large
front door to a Queen Ann-style country house. Sadly, the brackets,
along with the pediment and framework below, were stolen. The brackets
sat on columns below and supported a triangular pediment above, and
were fixed so the lions' heads were a little above eye level.

Unfortunately – and this is distressingly common – the client
could only offer a small, grainy and somewhat smudgy photocopy
of the originals. The replacements were therefore a mixture of what
the client remembered and what new features she wanted. In this
chapter, I describe how I constructed the brackets, and carved the
volute, leaves and the lion heads.

When you make a pair of anything, one question poses itself:
how close do they have to be in appearance? My view is that it
usually depends on how the objects will be seen. If they are close

together – such as candlesticks on a table – then they are easily compared and any difference noted. If the objects are well separated, for example bedposts, or these brackets, the close comparison is difficult and you can work a little more freely. The point it that, while attempting to make an identical pair, a lot of time can be wasted trying to make a precise match when such precision is redundant.

Construction

The sequence

Each bracket consisted of several parts: a large volute, flowers, foliage and leaves and a lion's head. These parts can be thought of separately; they were carved almost in sequence:

■ **Large volute:** A volute is a spiral; this gives the main bulge to the form. In this case, the volute was created by a simple square flute or trench to the side. Volutes can be much more three-dimensional, however.

■ **Flowers:** These were chosen by the client: rose, daffodil, thistle and shamrock – one for each side of the two brackets – which spilt from the ends of these trenches.

■ **Foliage:** Leaves, emerging over the top of the volute and below at the front.

■ **Lion's head:** At the base, from which the volute arises. There is an integral block above the volute that acts as a plinth for the pediment; it is smaller than the volute and has the effect of making the volute more dramatic.

The woodworker making the pediment and lower frame fixed the overall dimensions. The height 28in (710mm), width 7in (180mm) and depth 14in (355mm) – as well as the dimensions of the top and bottom ends which fitted pediment and frame – had to be exact. How much the carving projected as volute or lion was left to me.

Sketches

Work begins with pencil and paper – I like to start with many rough sketches. These preliminary sketches eventually work up into two full size drawings: a front view and a matching side view. It really is vital to work out as much beforehand as possible, to minimize the potential for mistakes. For the lions' heads, I needed to research lions, real and sculpted, and sketch heads both on paper and in clay. I also had to decide how the shapes of the foliage and flowers at the sides would work with the volute.

There are mathematical ways of drawing scrolls or volutes. I've never really got on with these; they often look a little heartless – too 'true' – for my taste. Instead, I opt for a freehand drawing: I draw a line again and again until it is heading in the right direction, refining and tracing as necessary. In this case I needed a spiral trench – so two lines. Once I have one line, one side of the trench, running 'just so', I space out the other. It actually took me less time than laying out a spiral geometrically, and was more fun!

The template

I glued a full-size, side-view drawing to thick cardboard and cut it out with a craft knife. This drawing thus became an accurate and vital full size template which would help me in three important ways. I could:

1 Draw an accurate outline for bandsawing. Then, once the outline was cut, I could draw my leaves, and so on, on the front.
2 Easily draw the paths of the volute trenches on to the wood.
3 Be sure that the brackets – and the sides of each bracket – were the same.

The brackets were to be made in English oak, to match the door and frame as well as for the wood's weathering qualities. To minimize the chance of splitting, I used thick, seasoned boards and laminated to size with exterior glue. Even though the boards were machine-planed, I went over them with a fine hand plane to ensure the tightest fit.

Right from the start my template came in useful: with its help I could place splits and knots in component boards, in parts of the carving I knew would be removed, or deep in the wood mass out of harm's way. To use a template like this, the starting block must be accurately machined, with square corners. I drew the outline of the whole work on both sides, checking that each side matched – 'registered'– by drawing lines across the front. I carefully marked the important plinth block at the top, making sure I wouldn't forget it!

Bandsawing

The bandsaw is the tool of choice; the alternative is crosscutting and chopping the wood out – a very long task. I needed to bandsaw from both sides of the wood. The throat of my saw is not large enough to take this size of work from one side and so some planning is necessary.

Cutting from both sides would be impossible without accurate squared blocks of wood and matching outlines of the bracket, on both sides. It's worth taking the trouble to register the outlines well. I removed some big chunks of wood first in order to get closer to my outline, then refined my cuts until I had an accurate profile.

Carving the side

The carving broke down into neat parts. I worked each side of the brackets in turn first, with the piece resting on the workbench. Then, for the front, I mounted it vertically on an adjustable bench.

The volute

I used the template again to draw the internal lines of the volute, pinning it to the wood and truing up the lines when it was removed: smooth, flowing and parallel █.

1 I've already used my master template to give a correct profile to the block; here I'm using it to mark out the lines of the volute.

2 Lining in the volute trench with a V tool. Note how I am running the groove so that the side cutting against the grain is to the waste.

3 Excavating the trench with a fluter – a U-shaped gouge.

4 Setting in the walls of the trench prior to cleaning and flattening the bottom.

The work consisted of removing a spiral trench or 'flute', accurately. I angled the walls of this trench slightly to catch a little light. I could gauge the depth or the trench from where the background was free, to the rear. I began with a large 60° V tool (No 39) to 'line in' on the waste side of my spiral lines. As you cut diagonally across grain with a V tool, one side cuts with the grain, the other against. This meant I always had to cut with the 'good' side of the V tool against my line, and the 'bad' to the waste **2**.

Once round, I followed with a U-shaped gouge (No 11) to remove waste wood, repeating V and U tools until I arrived at my depth **3**. I set in the walls of the trench with wide flat gouges, and cleaned the bottom with similar, bent tools – remembering that the flowers rise from the floor of the trench at the outer end, therefore to keep spare wood here. To finish, I removed the pencil lines with a sanding block; checked the corners and adjusted the edges **4**.

Side flowers and foliage

The flowers – rose, daffodil, thistle and shamrock – which arise from the trench flutes were bold and simple in design, to be viewed from a distance. I'll only show the carving of the thistle here, which follows the standard pattern for relief carving. I drew out the thistle, and its leaf, on to the wood. The space that the flowers filled was roughly triangular, so the shape of the thistle, our example, was adapted to suit. There are three different levels to consider: the thistle itself, which is the highest point, the background, furthest back and the leaf, in between **5**.

After lining in the thistle itself with a V tool, I began clearing the wood away down to the leaf below **6**. I then redrew the leaf, lined it in, and took the surrounding wood back to the background itself using 'grounders' – short, bent, flat gouges **7**. I set in tidily and, lastly, modelled the thistle and leaf, adding the details **8**.

Carving the front

The sides of the brackets were finished and I could turn to the front – first fitting the woodcarver's screw so I could hang the workpiece from my vertical carving stand **9**.

To begin, I cleaned up the area between these top, high relief leaves and those below – the ones arising from behind the lion's head. For this I used a flat gouge and set-square. I carefully defined the edge of the volute. I established the overall shape and masses of the leaves first. The centre portion remains high and the leaves roll over to the sides. Then I followed the simple shaping and detailing. A moderate undercut gave them shadow **10**. The spaces between the leaves were cleaned up with a skew chisel **11**.

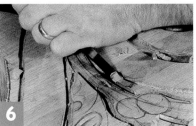

5 Drawing in the first set of flowers and leaves: a thistle; their stems must slope down into the floor of the trench.

6 Separating flowers from leaves.

7 The leaves have been set in and now I am finishing the surrounding background.

8 Modelling the leaves.

Top leaves

Now for the top, low relief leaves. Below the large leaves spilling over the top of the volute hung a small three-leaved clover. The cloverleaf was a simple light or low relief carving. I found turning the carving upside down on its holding screw the easiest way to work with the grain – in other words, 'downhill' **12**.

After drawing and lining in with the V tool I lowered and levelled the background, set in the outline and modelled the surface. I had to take care keep the background level flat relative to the surface of the volute **13**.

Lower leaves

Next the high relief leaves. Last of the foliage was the large feather-like leaf which arises from behind the lion's head. First the whole leaf had to be carved into its rough shape **14**. The main vein and divisions on the inside were carefully drawn using my working drawings as a guide **15**. I separated the lobes on the flattish 'inside' with the V tool, before shaping and modelling them and leading them into the underside of the 'curl'. The trickiest lobe was the one halfway between the flat and curl: a transitional shape that makes sense of the whole leaf **16**. The outer, top aspect of the leaves was carved to reflect the shaping underneath. I wanted to maintain the interesting curl **17**. I needed a backbent gouge to round over the central vein. I found, again, that being able to rotate the carving was essential for gaining access to various parts **18**.

9 Side view of the bracket showing the finished volute and thistle. Note the large woodcarver's screw with which I will hold the brackets for the next stage of carving, to its front.

10 Top leaves, roughly divided up into component parts.

11 After modelling, I lightly undercut the leaves. Here the skew chisel comes into its own.

12 The cloverleaf is a simple low relief. Having lined it in with a V tool, I am removing the background.

13 Finished cloverleaf; everything must be kept simple.

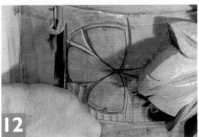

30 The mane was started with a V tool, then sharpened up and cut further with gouges.

31 Profile of a lions' mane, eyes and mouth.

32 Finished lion's head, front view.

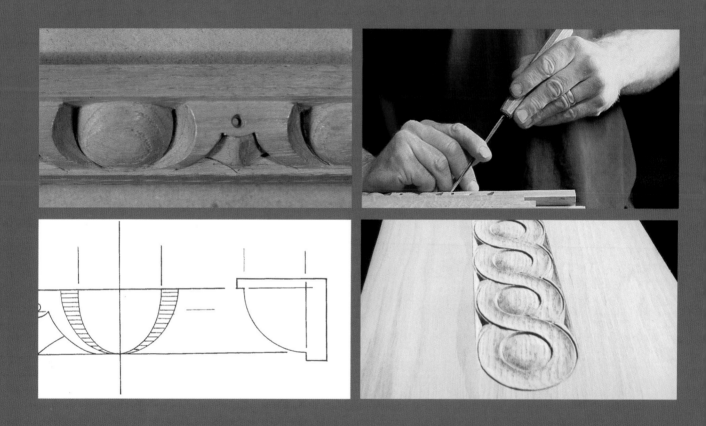

Part Three
Moulding

- **Waterleaf Moulding**

- **Egg and Dart Moulding**

- **Acanthus Leaf Moulding**

- **Guilloche Moulding**

Waterleaf Moulding

In the following chapters I will demonstrate some common and useful mouldings in their simpler forms: waterleaf, egg and dart, acanthus and guilloche. Along with information on how to do the carving, I will discuss the use and design of mouldings and how professional carvers approach this sort of work.

▲ Detail from the waterleaf moulding.

Plain mouldings present distinct bands of light and shadow. A second level of decoration can be added by carving rhythmic patterns, giving a huge number of possibilities and potential mixtures. Mouldings may be geometrically simple or complex; plain or carved, wide or narrow, used singly or built up. Carved mouldings always start from the plain, unadorned moulding in the appropriate section, so running this is always the first job. Carve mouldings separately and then apply them where possible. Any mistakes are then limited to the piece of moulding. It is far more difficult to get at 'stuck' or integral mouldings, especially internal ones, for example, working round a fielded panel.

Mouldings divide into two main types – architectural and furniture. Architectural mouldings are historically older and found in cornices, architraves or fireplaces, in stone and wood. They are larger and bolder, and often assembled into elaborate, compound patterns. There is much overlap in design, so observe architectural mouldings and see how common furniture mouldings can be seen within them.

Furniture mouldings are smaller, usually simpler (although they can be as elaborate as architectural work) runs of pattern contrasting with plain areas of mouldings. Furniture mouldings are usually seen close up, and should be placed so the carving can be seen as much as possible. I have designed exercise mouldings for carving into a specific moulding section with specific tools. The following chapters illustrate some general principles in the layout and carving of all mouldings.

The egg and dart moulding

Most of our mouldings have their origins in ancient Greek or Roman architecture. The egg and dart moulding can be seen in ancient Athens and probably has something to do with life and death. Egg and dart is always carved into an ovolo (from the Greek 'egg-like') section moulding.

The ovolo is an arc of a circle but can be rounder or flatter depending on where the centre is placed. A true quarter circle, as here, gives a stronger appearance. The curve shows off more of the work. This is more intimate, more suitable for furniture. A flatter ovolo is more often used in larger, wider, architectural mouldings. It is less strong in appearance but effective from a distance when mixed with other carved moulding. It is easier to carve as less wood needs to be removed. A flattened ovolo could be used on the edge of a large table, for example.

Part No.	A	B	C	D	E	F
T1339 ½	12.7mm	23mm	½	36mm	41.4mm	12.5mm

Moulding tips

Mouldings need to be crisply carved to look their best. Carvers use the word 'spontaneity'. The rules for achieving this are:
• The fewer tools the better.
• Use as few cuts as possible, at best only one.
• Use the same tool for as long as possible before changing.
• Cut consistently, at the same angle and to the same depth, each time.

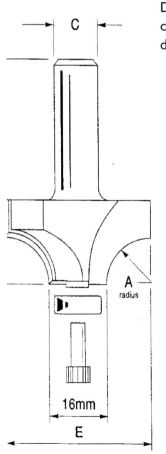

Details of the Wealden ovolo cutter used for the egg and dart moulding.

The ovolo section moulding used for egg and dart is a quarter circle. If the centre of the circle is offset then a flatter ovolo results.

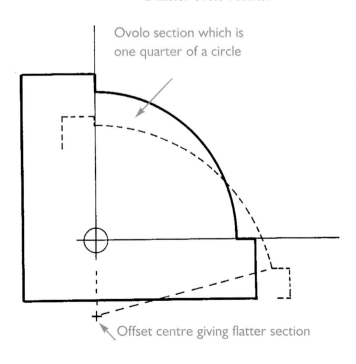

Ovolo section which is one quarter of a circle

Offset centre giving flatter section

Preparation

For this exercise I used a Wealden cutter, part No T1339 ½ which has a radius of ½in (12.7mm), giving a profile of a ¼ circle. The arrangement of a piece of practice wood is the same as for the waterleaf moulding in the last chapter, see page 56.

Tools

For the egg and dart moulding the following tools are needed (see Sheffield List page 162 and Pfeil system page 164):
No 6 x 20mm
No 6 x 14mm
No 9 x 3mm
Fishtail No 4 x 8mm
Fishtail No 6 x 18mm
These tools should be correctly and immaculately sharp.

Setting out

Eye line

This line is drawn in a similar way to the one for the waterleaf moulding in the last chapter – using either a template or your finger as a guide against the wall of the top fillet . Draw the eye line about a third of the way from the wall down the curve of the ovolo section. As before, the eye is actually placed above this line.

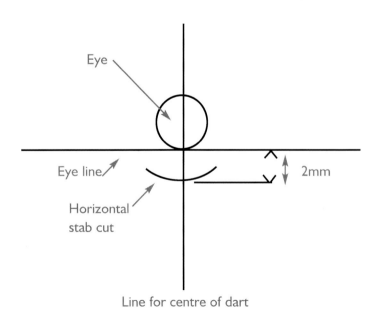

Eye

Eye line

Horizontal
stab cut

2mm

Line for centre of dart

1 Drawing the outlines of the egg using a template made of thin flexible plastic.

2 Stab cuts on the lines . . .

3 . . . followed by angled cuts . . .

4 . . . give the embryonic outline of the egg.

Position the eye on the eye line and symmetrically about a vertical. Estimate the horizontal stab cut by eye, leaving about ⁵⁄₆₄in (2mm) between it and the eye.

Stepping off

The unit of repetition is shown in the drawing. The divisions stepped off for carving with compass or dividers are a length equal to the radius, in this case ½in (12.5mm). Each division is a quarter of the full unit of repetition and establishes key points in the carving: eyes and darts, centre and width of eggs.

Vertical lines

Draw these, through the points stepped off, using a flexible piece of card as with the waterleaf.

Egg outlines

The exact outlines of the egg. In this case they fit the No 7 x 20mm gouge. Use this gouge to cut another piece of flexible plastic as a template. Different sizes of egg must be worked out on a bit of scrap wood first. The curve of the gouge will span the moulding at the correct profile. Use the template to mark in the left and right sides of the eggs. Remember to leave two divisions between each egg.

Carving

The carving is done in two parts. First the eggs are finished, then the darts.

Egg outlines

Place the No 6 x 20mm gouge vertical to the moulding and, with a mallet, stab first the left outlines, then the right. The cutting edge should stretch from the wall at the top fillet to the lowermost part of the egg curve. As the cutting edge is flat while the section of the moulding is convex, the cut will be deepest in the middle, feathering out to nothing in the corners **2**.

Angled cuts

Using the No 6 x 20mm gouge, two angled cuts, made from alternate sides of the egg with a mallet, define its outline ready for the next stage of shaping. Estimate the maximum width of the curved waste chip of wood by eye at ⅛in (3mm). Work either one side of the egg along the whole moulding, or on alternate sides. You may have to repeat the vertical cut to remove the waste cleanly which will be deep in the middle **3**.

Shape the top two-thirds of the egg

Again use the No 6 x 20mm gouge. I find it best to shape the egg in two parts, the smaller, lower part of the egg needing a smaller gouge **4**.

5 Shape the sides of the top part of the eggs...

6 ... and continue the cut up to the top wall below the fillet.

7 Cleaning the top triangular corners.

Profile

Gouges in the upside down position will naturally produce the convex profile of the egg. On hard wood you may need a mallet, but you must finish off by hand to give a smooth surface to the egg.

- Start on the left side of the egg.
- Place the left corner of the tool in the crescent-shaped cut with the handle low.
- Push the gouge forward and round to shape the egg, up to the top wall **5**.
- You will probably need to repeat the previous angled cut to clean down to a neat root in the trench outlining the egg.
- Repeat on the other side, merging the cuts to give a smooth egg surface, and pushing up to the top wall at the fillet **6**.

Top end triangles

With the No 6 x 20mm, finish off the top ends of the crescents at the wall below the fillet with the corner of the gouge while you still have it in your hand. Or you can use the No 4 x 8mm fishtail gouge **7**.

Shape the lower one-third of the egg

You may be able to use the 20mm tool and include this carving in the previous work. Otherwise use the No 6 x 14mm gouge **8**.

- Sweep the gouge around the lower part of the egg, shaping it while merging it with the rest.
- Clean up the root of the curving side trench, the junction where the angled walls and the sides of the egg meet.

The egg is now finished. Make sure everything is crisp and neat before moving on **9**. You should have found the drawn centre line a guide to symmetry. It can be lightly skimmed off, while removing flats on the egg surface, but the ovolo profile must be left unscathed. There should be no sanding.

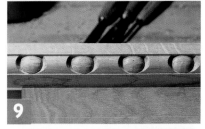

8 The bottom part of the egg, being of smaller curvature, often needs a smaller tool to shape and clean it up. But it is also possible to cut the whole egg with the larger tool, sweeping the corner tightly round.

9 A completed row of eggs.

10 Rotate the gouge to produce the eyes...

11 ...and punch them down with a flattened nail.

12 A stab cut beneath the eye with the fishtail gouge.

Darts

Eyes

Place the eye above the line in the centre of the stepped vertical.

- These are cut by rotating the No 9 x 3mm gouge into the wood until a pip jumps out **10**.
- Punch the eyes with a flattened nail to lower them further and level their bases **11**.

Horizontal and side crescents

This work must be done by eye, but you will see how the size and shape of the tools makes the outcome fairly inevitable.

- With the No 4 x 8mm fishtail gouge, stab a horizontal cut symmetrically below the eyes leaving a 2mm space between **12**.
- With the No 6 x 14mm gouge stab vertically down from the corner of the horizontal cut to feather out at the bottom of the ovolo. First one side, then the other.
- These cuts define the crescent to the side of the egg, an untouched area of the original moulding surface. Do not undercut **13**.
- Remove a curve of wood from each side with the No 6 gouge, first from one side, then the other **14**.

Dart ends

The carving here is more or less the same as for the waterleaf moulding in the previous chapter.

- With the No 4 x 8mm fishtail, stab the right lower side of the crescent edges of the dart, taking care not to stab into the wood below the horizontal **15**.
- Stab the left side of the dart to its mid-line point **16**.
- A horizontal cut will now remove a chip of wood to reveal the outline of the dart **17**.
- Work your way along the moulding making these three neat chip cuts.

Shape dart

With the fishtail or No 6 gouge make a sloping cut to each side of the dart, first to the left, then the right to finish off the dart.

Summary

The egg and dart moulding, in this simple form, is now complete. There is much more to learn, such as: the centring of the pattern and how to treat corners, and there are countless mouldings out there to explore. But you should have little problem once you have the hang of working with the tools, and a proper examination of examples will give you an idea of what you need to do.

13 Stab cuts to the edge of the crescent...

14 ...and angled cuts to remove the wood chip.

15 The darts are profiled...

16 ...then the tip of the dart...

17 ...and a horizontal cut to remove the waste.

Acanthus Leaf Moulding

This enduring and attractive design has been used and adapted countlessly throughout the ages and makes a useful addition to any carver's repertoire.

▲ Simple acanthus moulding.

Acanthus leaves must be the commonest foliage design that carvers use for decoration. First introduced by the Greeks, and modified by every Western culture from the Romans to rococo, it is small wonder the artistic, artificial acanthus we know bears little resemblance to the original plant. A common and principal adaptation that characterizes acanthus leaves is the way veins and side leaves are made to run parallel and flow from the main stem, rather than emerging abruptly at an angle. This gives the leaf a wonderful liquid quality that is the reason for both its popularity and its ready adaptability. Here, we will look at a simple acanthus leaf moulding.

It is easy to see the repeat pattern or unit of the moulding: main leaves, subdivided, and dart-like leaves in between. This is similar to the waterleaf moulding shown on page 54. People often need large amounts of carved moulding and it is only fair to warn you that this repetitive carving can be tedious. It takes a certain mental perseverance that few people possess in abundance. To me, the rhythm of cutting a moulding is rather like knitting – and the stamina needed can feel like a marathon. Imagine carving long mouldings to be like running a marathon while knitting.

Once you have worked out your pattern of tool use and got the hang of any moulding, you need to quickly get into a rhythmic, almost meditative, state of mind. Work evenly and set yourself a comfortable amount to carve every day. I find music a great help.

Tool control

Next to letter carving, mouldings are probably the quickest way to learn tool control, so are worth attempting as an exercise. For successful carving of more complicated mouldings you need to understand how carving tools cut, as well as noticing the way you are carving. There are several habits to avoid.

The wedge effect

The bevel (inside plus outside) of any carving tool is nothing less than a wedge of metal and as such will prise apart wood fibres. The effect can be disastrous and is the usual cause of bits falling off, not just of mouldings but of carvings in general.

To avoid this happening:

- ■ Be conscious of where the short and weak grain lies.
- ■ Use lighter, thinner tools, especially fishtails.
- ■ Grind or benchstone off the bevel corners (see diagram, right).
- ■ Push only as deep as you need. You may need to push in only the corner, rather than the whole width of the cutting edge, stabbing in and levering the corner across.
- ■ Never wobble or agitate the tool in the cut. Come straight out the way you went in.
- ■ If you cannot cut as deeply as you wish in one go, because of the danger of wedging out short grain, just stab as deep as you dare for now, returning to the cut later for a second stab after surrounding waste has been cleared.
- ■ On the positive side, you can use the wedge effect when setting in to jump out tight, awkward corners of short grain. This will be seen with the crescents (see diagram, below right).

When cutting:

- ■ Stab to the required depth safely, precisely, uniformly and consistently.
- ■ You can leave light stab marks at junctions, but these should be moderate and consistent.
- ■ There is a tendency, hard for beginners to avoid, to make left and right hand cuts differently. Be on the lookout for this and strive for symmetry.
- ■ Keep cuts vertical to the wood surface. It is rare for elements in mouldings to be undercut.
- ■ Work forwards, with the tools leading your body, rather than backwards.
- ■ Build up the cuts with a consistent angle and depth.
- ■ Leave all cuts clean as you proceed. There should be no tidying up needed at the end, so finish as you go along.
- ■ Use a stiff brush to clear away shavings and debris occasionally.
- ■ Because the surface you are cutting into is curved (it has a profile) sometimes initial stabbing needs a series of taps with the mallet, necessarily raising or lowering the tool handle to set in along the line.

Preparation

The section used for this moulding is shown in the drawing on page 68. It gives the repeat unit I worked with. As with most foliage mouldings, including the waterleaf, the section is cyma reversa, the so-called roman or reverse ogee.

When setting up, I held the lengths of moulding at the same angle as before, but instead of wedges I used a few dabs of hot glue on the back. When the carving was done I prized off the strip with a chisel or spatula. The cold hot glue more or less peeled away. Make sure you are working at a comfortable height.

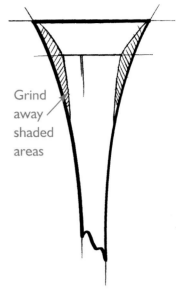

Removing the bevel corners makes the sides of the cutting edge thinner and less likely to break grain through the wedge effect.

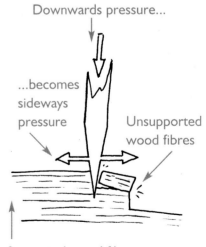

The bevel of a carving tool acts as a wedge as it is pushed into the wood, easily breaking weak grain.

Laying out the acanthus leaf

Setting out with the template is more an aide-memoire than a plan
to slavishly follow. Carving tool sweeps make precise shapes, far more
accurate and consistent than your drawing. It is the tool cuts you should
work to, and which give the liveliest result. With practice and confidence
it is possible to cut with only a few guide marks to unit length.

   Lay out the design by stepping off units and then drawing the outline
of the leaves with a prepared template, working to corners or returns.
When it comes to fitting in the repeat units of any moulding to individual lengths of wood, remember that if you change the width of a unit by
a tiny amount, ten units later you will have gained or lost much more.

The pattern and section, or
profile, of the moulding used.

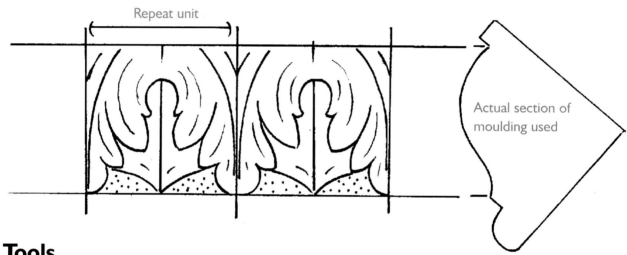

Tools

As near as I can tell, comparing with the Sheffield list (see page 162), the
tools I used (but not in this order) were:

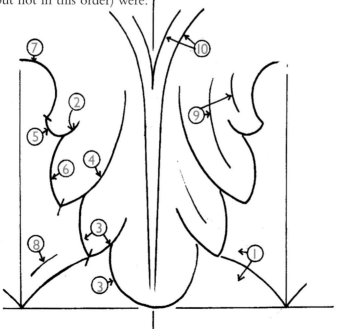

1. No 3 x 8mm
2. No 6 x 6mm
3. No 6 x 8mm
4. No 6 x 22mm
5. No 8 x 5mm
6. No 8 x 8mm
7. No 8 x 10mm
8. No 10 x 3mm
9. No 11 x 2mm
10. No 39 x 5mm

The drawing shows the
approximate places the tools
were used. You may have to
match your own tools by
adjusting the leaf design.

Layout

This guilloche is 4in (100mm) wide and a length which seemed to go on for a long time. The width is a good one for working with, but you can make it a different size if it suits you. It can be as long as your patience allows.

Stages in the layout are shown in the drawing below. Use a planed-up plank of fairly tight-grained wood and score with a marking gauge two parallel lines that mark the width of the guilloche track. If this is more than an exercise, you need to give some thought to how the circles relate to the required length, and how the ends finish.

I ended in a round band, in which case the gauge marks must stop short of the end of the board – but you can end squarely with two end triangles. You can also make the widths of the bands themselves wider or narrower. In the band there is a repeating crossing over of one band by the other, you need to decide which way it is going. If you are making two lengths of the guilloche, you can have bands crossing in opposite directions.

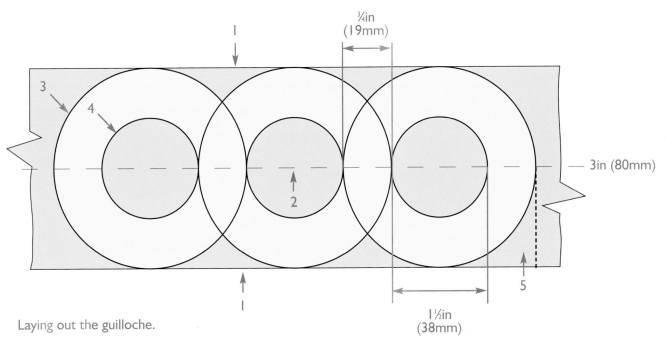

Laying out the guilloche.
1 Mark top and bottom lines
2 Pencil centre line. Step off circle centres
3 Draw outside circles
4 Then inner circles
5 Corners at ends may be carved

Grain

Note that the grain, or fibres of wood, go along the plank – along the guilloche. In this exercise, you are going to be going with the grain all the time 'downhill'. Think of how you sharpen a pencil with a knife. You cannot sharpen it away from the point. The drawing shows the way the wood must be cut to run with the grain – this is something to bear in mind throughout the exercise.

Tools

I used the following tools (see Sheffield list on page 162 and Pfeil system on page 164):

V tool x 6mm
Chisel x 8mm
No 4 gouge x 12.5mm
No 6 gouge x 12.5mm
No 6 gouge x 25mm
Mallet

The centre buttons

Start with the centre buttons. I would suggest you do one or two first to see what tools you need and depth to go to, then run the whole series of cuts with the same tool.

Take the larger medium gouge – one that has a sweep matching the curve of the button circumference – and stab in neatly around the perimeter using the mallet. Lean in a little ▮. Use the same gouge to follow the line around again from the inside, leaning out. This will produce a v-shaped, circular trench ▮.

Next, take the flatter gouge and cut from the left, the right, top and bottom to dome the button. You can take the bulk out with the mallet and finish off by hand. Swap hands with the tools to avoid an awkward posture. You will soon see there is only one way to get a clean cut. If necessary, you can clean up the edge of the button a little with the first gouge ▮. Use the small, firmer chisel to merge in any remaining flats on top of the button ▮.

1 First cut to centre button.

2 Top half of button, cutting with the grain this way.

3 Reversing to follow it, cutting 'downhill', on the opposite side.

4 Merging in any flats that might have been left.

Outlining the guilloches

Before you cut anything, decide which band is going to overlap which and how the lines go – you don't want to make a mistake – check twice, cut once. Use a V tool to run the line in sections, starting with the top half, then the lower half. You can use the mallet with light tapping if the wood is hard, chasing the lines by hand to finish. Make the lines smooth and arc-like – and if possible complete the curve in one clean stroke. This is a good exercise in its own right **5** and **6**.

When you have finished with the V tool, you will begin to see the ghostly forms of the guilloche. The V tool, as it makes a curving cut, will cut one side with the grain and the other against it. This leaves a shinier and rougher face in the groove. With this shallow depth of cut this may not be so apparent, but look carefully. You might need to reverse the direction of cut to clean the lines up.

Carving the bands

The bands themselves are hollow channels, flutes, contrasting with convex buttons. They don't have to be very deep to get the effect. Using the smaller, medium sweep gouge – which you will see is a little over half the width of the band – start making the cuts from the right, top and bottom. The first thing you will notice is that you can only cut half the width of each band at a time with the grain **7**. If the cutting edge of the gouge crosses the mid-line it is cutting against the grain on the other side.

5 Chasing the outline of the bands.

6 Take great care to get the overlap right.

Tip

You may like to work in batches of six or ten units to prevent boredom setting in – it is exacting work until you get the hang of it.

Direction of cutting

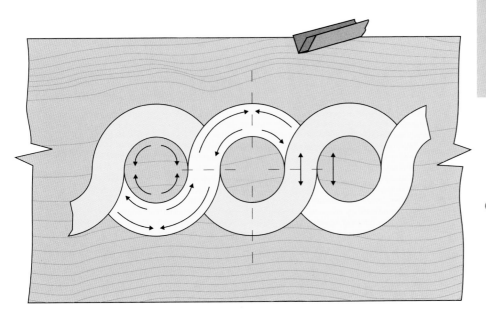

Grain direction in boards

As you pass into the part of the band curving in the opposite direction, you must, in effect 'cross the road' and work along the opposite half **8**. Reverse the direction of cut (in this case change to working from the left) and work the opposite halves of the bands. The two directions of cuts must be merged in the middle of the hollow **9** and **10**. This is less complicated when you have the wood in front of you, or if you study the drawing. I recommend you start your cuts from the centre where you are working across the grain. Use a mallet carefully to start with, finishing by hand. You will need to clean up at the crossover – the corner of the small chisel is useful here.

It is a good idea to swap hands for either direction. This way you can work with the grain without cranking your arms into a yoga position. When you have finished, reverse the wood to get a different view and tidy up any torn grain.

Learning about grain direction

After you have worked along the guilloche, you should have a good idea of how working with the grain means essentially cutting 'downhill'. This is evident as you sweep from top to bottom parts of the band. You will also have found how working across the grain – in the middle sections – is a very satisfactory option, providing you have sharp tools. Working against the grain can be done with very sharp tools, taking shallow cuts with a slicing action, in most tight-grained woods. The facet produced will always lack the shiny, polished finish of one cut in either of the other two directions. Cutting against the grain is usually seen as a last resort when you cannot get at the area from any other direction.

7 Cutting with the grain on the outer edge.

8 Crossing over on to the inner edge to keep cutting with the grain.

9 Only half the width of a band can be cut at a time.

10 Crossing over to continue cutting cleanly.

Cutting the triangles

When the curved band of the guilloche meets the straight line of the edge, a delta-like space is left. In the past this has been used to add some extra, interesting item such as stylized, or fan-shaped foliage. The same circumstance arises in Gothic tracery. In this instance, all that is required is a bit of chip carving to create a three-sided depression that adds interest by shadow. You still need to pay attention to the grain. Start by stabbing three lines from the centre of the triangle to the points. Using the corner of a firmer chisel, cut deeper in the centre, reaching the surface at the points. These are stop cuts which prevent the wood splintering out of control 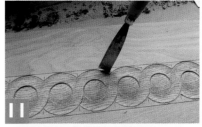. Using the corner of the flattish gouge used earlier or a fishtail version of it, make the side cuts, holding the gouge mouth down. Come from right and left again, swapping hands as before. Try and let the corner follow the stab line that you made with the chisel to maintain a uniform depth .

The third part of the triangle is taken out with the corner of the chisel, trying to marry the three faces together. After a few, you should be able to make these cuts without having to do more than touch up the joins. This last cut involves cutting along the grain, parallel with it. Even though your chisel may be very sharp, the grain of the wood is unlikely to be straight, bending a little one way and the other. This means that you may well find yourself cutting in the same direction – sometimes with the grain and sometimes against it when it splinters up in front of the cutting edge. You must be prepared to reverse the direction the chisel is cutting before tearing too much wood so you are able to make a clean cut .

A newcomer to carving will have experienced the constant need to be aware of the way the grain is running, and working with it in order to carve cleanly – gaining a sense of going with the grain. By the time a long length of it is finished, they will have benefitted from a lot of practice controlling their carving tools.

11 Stabbing 'stop cuts' to the centre of the triangular darts.

12 Swapping hands and cutting in the opposite direction, still with the grain.

13 Final cut to the dart along the grain – this can be tricky with wavy grain.

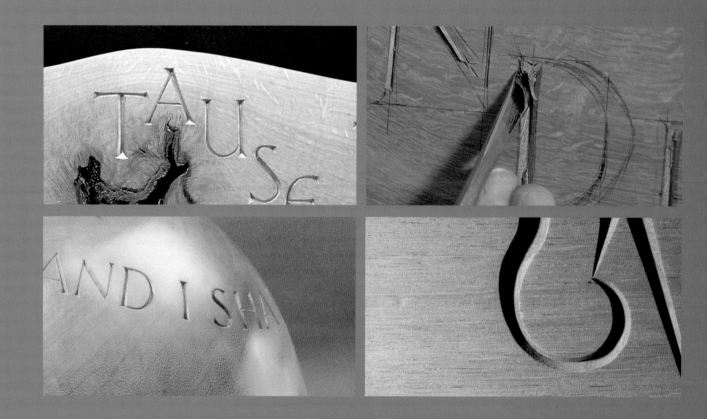

Part Four
Lettering

- **Perfect Prose**

- **Decorative House Sign**

- **Gilding the House Sign**

- **Peace Process**

- **Tibetan Tails**

Perfect Prose

Lettering is a challenge for all carvers of all abilities and requires practice. This chapter illustrates how to carve letters, using prose from a much-loved poem.

▲ The finished board –
'Tief und tausendfach zu leben'.

Planning a panel of lettering is a challenging undertaking. Not only must you be able to carve the letters themselves but you must also place them in a context. It is not enough just to carve one letter well – you have to carve them all well. A letter stroke that is thicker than those it is next to, for example, will stand out like a wrong note in a tune. When the same two letters or numbers stand next to each other they must be absolutely the same – the years 1999 and 2000 sorted out the sheep from the goats!

You need consistency, trueness of line and a bit of flair to make a good job of lettercarving. Carvers practising the exact and disciplined nature of lettering in wood find that other areas of their carving improve enormously. So, if you have never tackled lettering before and want to improve your carving, I would encourage you to have a go. My own book, *Lettercarving in Wood – A Practical Course* (see Recommended Reading on page 170) will start you off the right way.

Important though it is, cutting the letters themselves is only one aspect of lettercarving. In some ways, the layout is even more important – spacing and arranging the letters you carve. The important point is that a good layout can carry a less than perfect carving. If on the other hand the layout and design are both poor, no amount of tidy carving will make

Carving

It is best to think of the carving in two stages: first removing the bulk of the waste and then shaping and finishing the edges and walls. Use the biggest tools you have for both stages and, for a hard wood like this, a mallet where you can.

Removing the waste

You should seek to remove about 90% of the waste at this stage. Remember, all walls, including the end ones at the serifs, are at a 60° angle. Flat is best – don't 'belly' them, but a little hollowing is acceptable and probably inevitable where the walls run concave. Take your largest V tool and enter at the corners of the serifs. Run a big 'V' groove along the centre line of all the letters, going as deep as you can, but without burying the cutting edge . Pass in both directions and widen the groove by tilting the tool to favour the 'V' edge cutting with the grain. Use your eye to keep the centre line.

Turn to a deep gouge, say a No 8, and cut down the walls towards the root from both sides . Don't worry too much about creating a root at this stage, but do keep an eye on its eventual place in the centre. Repeat with the 'V' tool and gouge to drop the embryonic root further back . Think mid-line.

Switch to a medium gouge to clean up the walls, trying to keep them flat and at the correct angle. The trick here is that you are removing waste at a good rate still and, if you place the cutting facets just above where you judge the final wall to be, the next stage of dressing the walls and edges to a finish will be very quick. Work this way across all the letters, and as far as you can with the smaller elements.

Shaping and finishing

At this size, the letter walls will be slightly faceted and it would be impossible and pointless to make them truly flat. Indeed, when this sign is eventually gilded, the irregularity of the surface will help give the letters a little sparkle at a distance. However, this faceting should be unobtrusive and not affect the surface edges.

It might seem that the shapes of the letters will cause problems, but you'll soon see there is a logic to follow. Just keep the angle of the walls uniform and the movement and junctions will work out magically. With such a big trench you can clean the walls and junction in either of two ways: slicing down and along from above – the approach for more 'normal'-sized letters – and chasing along the letter, with the handle nearly parallel to the wood surface. This is a method usually more appropriate to stonecarving.

3 Run a big 'V' groove along the centre line of all the letters, going as deep as you can but not burying the cutting edge.

4 Cut down the walls towards the root from both sides using a deep gouge, for example a No 8.

5 … repeat with the V tool and gouge to drop the embryonic root further back.

Slicing

Choose a wide gouge that matches the curve of the letter at the surface and slice down the wall and along, paring with the grain **6**. The advantage of this approach is that you can match the sweep to the letter edge and obtain an immaculate outline.

Chasing

Use a chisel where the wall is convex and a flat gouge where concave. Slice as much as possible to maintain a clean surface **7**. Where the wall turns in a tight radius, use gouges 'upside down' and match the convex surface. To create the serif junctions use chisels, including a skew **8** . Don't forget that the centre point of a serif, where the end and sidewall meet, is deeper than the root along the letter body and forms, in effect, an inverted pyramid.

In this design, there were some acanthus leaf effects in the initial 'L'. I carved the walls of the 'L' at this point as if the leaves weren't there, and then led the leaves in smoothly with narrow, quick gouges **9**. Aim for the surface edges to be smooth and true, the root neat and centred, and the wall surfaces clean.

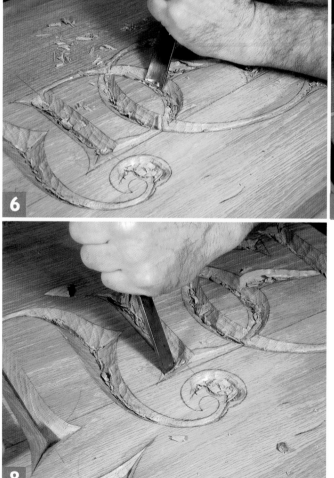

6 Slicing… using a wide gouge that matches the curve of the letter at the surface and slice down the wall and along, paring with the grain.

7 Chasing… use a chisel where the wall is convex, and a flat gouge where concave. To keep a clean surface, slice as much as possible.

8 To create the serif junctions use chisels, including a skew.

include more than just their heads – I wanted hearts and bodies to be involved in some way too. But how did one go about getting that 'extra'? For me it involved sitting quietly with the line 'And I shall have some peace now', trying to sense what it might mean to me if it were 'mine', and assessing how I might express whatever that sense was in the simplest way possible. The most important thing I wanted to avoid was sentimentalism or kitsch.

My response was that the words seemed to point to the end of a journey, where a 'peace' is found, and that the poet was coming to the conclusion upon some realization, some experience. Lastly – and here it becomes entirely personal – any peace we find, however far we journey, can only ever be here and now, this moment, deep within and beneath the daily surface. But how could I make these points and lead the viewer on this sort of discovery?

I turned to paper, pencil and modelling clay to help my ruminations but, in the end, examined my store of wood to see if any of my ideas fitted with available blocks and lumps. At some point – and to me this is one of the greatest mysteries – there was a creative 'aha!' The gong of inspiration struck, just like that. Even though I'd be adapting to what I'd find in the wood as I went along, I knew when I saw the lump of wood that I had, at last, found my way.

The wood

My co-source of inspiration was a block of iroko (*Chlorophora excelsa*) which has something of the working qualities and the interlocking, yellow-brown, coarse grain of teak . I obtained the block from the widow of a sculptor many years back, who had brought it into the country some 50 years ago. It was very dry and, thankfully, lacked the irritant dust that arises with newer iroko.

The block was roughly a 23½in (600mm) cube straight from the centre of the tree, the core of which was decayed and filled with cement-like stone. Little white flecks of this inclusion, nothing other than hardened chalk, appeared throughout the wood and would normally dull the edges of carving tools. Luckily I only used these for the lettering itself. There was also a split from end to end of the block. All these 'defects' had to be incorporated into the carving; indeed, I had to turn them into strengths.

This was a hefty block at around 30-40lbs/cubic foot (330-460kg/m3) and I needed a small block and tackle to lift it onto the bench. I knew the shape was going to resemble a pebble/egg – simple, smooth and tricky to hold. If you begin with a similar sized block of wood, make a triangular frame from 4 x 4in (100 x 100mm) timber so it binds nicely to the shape whichever way it is orientated. Pad the inner edges with leather to help grip – the sheer weight will keep the block in place. For the lettering, use a belt clamp around the sculpture and the bench – it is imperative that the block stays still.

1 The original and very heavy block, once the property of a sculptor in the 1950s, being lifted onto the bench.

2 Use a portable circular saw to remove as much of the corners as you can. A chainsaw is another option.

3 Use the Arbortech to reduce the original cube to something like an egg, leaning to one side losing symmetry.

Shaping

I differentiate through the distinctive tools and approach, and without a value judgment, 'shaping' and 'carving'. This sculpture involved both ways of working, starting with shaping and then sand power **2** . Cut into the block with an Arbortech to seek the round pebble-like shape. I dislike the dust and noise, but the speed at which work can be roughed out is well worth it **3** .

An important aspect of the carving is the feel; I wanted the viewer to lay on hands. However, the Arbortech is a very distant way of working as the power gets in between you and the wood. Once the form is established switch to a coarse Japanese (Shinto) saw rasp, and work all over the surface by hand, feeling and refining the surface as you go along so it flows smoothly **4** .

Once happy with the result use a drum sander on your drill. You can buy this at a DIY store: a sponge cylinder on an arbor. It is actually quite a responsive tool. The 'give' in the drum allows you to marry passes sensitively with little need for hand finishing **5** . At the end of this first stage I was left with a tactile, smooth egg, orientated off-centre and, due to the way the wood was, a split right down one face.

My idea was to lead the viewer around the smooth block to a cavity, a 'nest' in which they would find something after a journey, as implied by the text. I planned to fill the nest with glorious blue marbles. I built my nest directly out of the split, turning the straight crack into a shape like a drop of water. I drew the outline of the cavity in chalk, directly on the wood **6** .

I bored out a lot of the waste with a wide flat bit on my power drill, then consolidated and deepened the space with cutters and burrs on a high-speed flexible shaft – not a carving tool in sight. I deliberately left the inside of the nest rough and matt, sinking it deep into the middle of the wood **7** . I also re-cut the edges of the recess to raise a 'lip', which I had to blend in with the surrounding body of wood. Finally, to complete the shaping work, I stained the inside of the nest black with calligrapher's ink to increase the sense of depth and mystery further **8** .

The lettering

Without a doubt, the lettering is the trickiest part – this is where sharp gouges and chisels of carving proper become really useful. The whole project rests on the lettering. I wanted to start the line of text near the centre fault at the top and wind it down and around, to swoop up as it came to an end at the nest on the opposite side. This lift at the end is vital; a downward spiral could take the text down below mid-line eye level or, at the least, bestow a somewhat damping tone on the words. The letters took some planning. I chose a large loose Roman; formal enough to give authority to the text while still remaining quite 'friendly'.

4 Refine the form with a coarse rasp.

5 Sand the surface smooth.

6 The crack goes right through to the heart of the block but does not affect the strength. Here I am drawing in the outline of the 'nest'.

7 I left the inside of the cavity with a rough pattern to contrast with the smoothness of the contents. I have raised a 'lip' in the opening, which must be blended with the wood around.

Letters are constructed between two lines – the 'header' and 'footer'. Run a line of masking tape representing the header around the wood from where the text is to start and where it is to end. Measure this to get the length of the words. On paper, lay out the arrangement of letters and spaces to fit this length, playing with different options of letter height. Draw a second line parallel to the header line all the way around as the footer. Carefully transfer the letters from paper to wood using a white watercolour pencil and make careful adjustments to allow for the curved surface of the wood and how they feel in situ. This layout has to be done right before you even think of picking up a chisel 9 .

Actually carving the letters is straightforward. The only thing to note is that letters carve a lot easier when the grain runs horizontal because the bigger elements can be cut across it. Here the grain ran vertically – as if I needed more problems 10 .

It is very easy to feel pressured and make a mistake in this sort of delicate, 'just so' work. I find the best answer to this stress is simply to concentrate fully on cutting the letter in hand and having confidence in your layout. Rather like a musician, or an actor on stage, you can't afford to think of mistakes or how long you have in which to make one – you just have to make each moment right.

Painting and finishing

I painted the text in glossy, blue enamel, the sort used for plastic models 11 . I'd already decided that the contents of the nest were blue. I chose the letter colour to introduce the idea before the reader arrives at the nest. Sand, dampen and re-sand the main form very smooth before you begin the lettering. This way it will take very little work to crisp up the painting and restore the surface.

Finish the wood in simple beeswax, bringing out the colour in contrast with the blue of the letters. I also tinted the edges of the cavern with a touch of gilt wax and filled the nest with shiny, beautiful blue marbles. Why marbles? Everything in this sculpture had to work together: the spiralling flow of the text; the solid, simple shape suggesting an earthy strength; the direction of the text, leading the eye and hand around to the cave; the sense of discovery and, in the end, the desire to reach in and take out something 'precious' from deep within. It had to be something you'd hold up to the light, and blue is such an expansive, sky colour.

Whether the viewer actually 'understands the point' is not up to me. It is this combination of ideas, feelings and responses that makes this carving a sculpture – 'art' rather than 'craft'. Craft would be more the beautiful but straightforward rendition of the text. Art attempts to add that extra dimension to the communication, the personal response or reaction to the text. That's what I love about woodcarving: these edges are blurred and the possibilities endless.

8 I masked off the surrounding wood and stained the inside of the cavity with calligraphy ink and sealed with a U-V blocking, matt acrylic varnish.

9 White pencil lets you see the lines more clearly on the dark wood.

10 Carve the letters. You can see the strap clamp that holds the wood firmly.

11 Paint the letters. It is inevitable that some paint goes onto the surrounding wood.

◀ The finished character: Om.

Tibetan Tails

Basic lettercarving techniques can be applied to any alphabet or language as demonstrated with these Tibetan symbols that convey a well-known Buddhist mantra.

I believe there are common skills, or methods of working, in all aspects of carving. Once mastered these can be applied to a wide range of circumstances as they arise. This is just as true of lettercarving, and I thought I would try to demonstrate it by carving a short text in a language I could neither read nor write. Although I have occasionally come across Tibetan through my interest in Buddhism, I know nothing of its history, construction, or even how to pronounce it.

Other alphabets

Two problems immediately arise. The first is that not all alphabets, those derived from pen or brush, carve well in the sense of allowing carvers their normal intelligent cutting. The carver sometimes has to modify brush and pen forms to take into account the different way carving works. This I had to do with the Tibetan letters, to allow gouges and chisels to cut efficiently.

This brings about the second issue, which has to do with aesthetics. I might be pleased with my results in Tibetan, but what would a letterer from that culture think? Different cultures have varying aesthetic values, and not being familiar with the culture it may be that my interpretation of the letter forms would be seen as poor, or missing much beauty by those who are at home in it, although not by me of course. Having someone knowledgeable to criticize would have been a great help but, lacking this, a close study of examples was called for and I compared as many examples of this text as I could. Even so, I expect mistakes could easily be made. In such a case you have to decide whether to have a go or not, trusting in your aesthetic judgment. Then you wait for someone to criticize it, and do better next time.

However you decide to treat unfamiliar forms, it is important to be consistent and let the qualities of family resemblance, trueness of line, and balance of optical colour be your guide. And the chances are you will not be far out. The text I have taken is a mantra which is reasonably well known in the West since the Tibetan Diaspora, although not so much in its original Tibetan script: Om Mani Padme Hum.

The first character, Om, used as an example of applied lettercarving techniques.

The Tibetan mantra, Om Mani Padme Hum.

Looking for patterns

The first thing I look for are obvious patterns in the characters:

- The symbols hang below a strong line, rather than sit on one.

- There is a vertical stress. In other words the thinnest sections of the curves lie vertically above each other.

- There are horizontal blocks, curving and straight elements, repeating forms of fluid loops, and tapered straight elements, many of which are of uniform length.

The next thing was to fit the characters into a framework unifying the shapes and sizes of similar elements. I am taking a sample syllable from the text, the first one, Om, to make the point and show the basic techniques in action. You will need straight chisels and gouges. A fishtail chisel and gouge are very useful for the serifs and end walls.

Lay out the guiding lines and draw in the syllable on a medium density hardwood, with the grain running horizontal. Incise the vertical strokes first with a flat chisel. Start with a centre stop cut and then remove each angled side **1**. To remove a tapering wedge of a chip which will give the correct form, deepen the stop cut and angle cuts towards the top **2**.

Run stop cuts into the top corners of the right-hand stroke and shape the serif with the fishtail gouge and chisel. Incise the small horizontal bar at the top line with the fishtail chisel. Put in stop cuts at the ends first to stop the grain tearing out **3**. Incise the smaller tapering stroke in the same way as the larger vertical ones, bringing it into the cross bar. At the same time finish off the long tapering stroke into the bar **4** and **5**.

The straight sections of the character are now finished. In practice, and with a longer text, all elements which could be carved with one tool would be, before putting down the tool.

Curved parts

Now turn to the curved parts. Put in stop cuts to the centre of the curves using a gouge approximately the sweep of the outside line. Note how I have only roughly joined them together, but adequately for the purpose **6**. Sweep the same gouge round to incise the outside angled wall as far as you can. Use a slightly flatter gouge to run the inside angle cut **7**. You will need to reverse the gouges to merge the cuts along the walls **8**. Finish the end wall to the curve elements with the fishtail chisel and gouge **9**.

The body of the syllable is now finished. The last details are the top strokes and crescent and the little circle. These upper free forms and crescent are incised in a similar fashion to the curves: a centre stab cut and two angle cuts to remove the chip, and finishing off the ends with fishtails. For the small circle, run vertically around the line with a small gouge first, in this case a No 9 which is semicircular **10**. Follow with a slightly flatter gouge and take out a circular chip around the outside **11**. The character is now finished. A lot of the appearance must depend on fluidity of line and cleanliness of cutting.

1 Incising the tapered uprights.

2 Finishing the serif-like ends with fishtail tools.

3 Removing the horizontal block section.

4 Smaller tapered uprights carved in a similar way to the longer ones.

5 Finishing the uprights into the horizontal block.

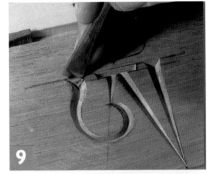

6 Stab cuts to the centre of curved elements.

7 Cutting the outer angled cuts. Sweep the gouge round, keeping the leading edge clear.

8 Lead the inner angle cuts as far round as possible. Reverse the gouges to match the curvature of the shape and merge cuts.

9 Finishing the end walls with a fishtail gouge.

10 A circular stab cut with a No 9 semicircular gouge. Be careful not to exert too much pressure or the centre will jump out.

11 An outside angled cut with a slightly flatter gouge will produce the circle.

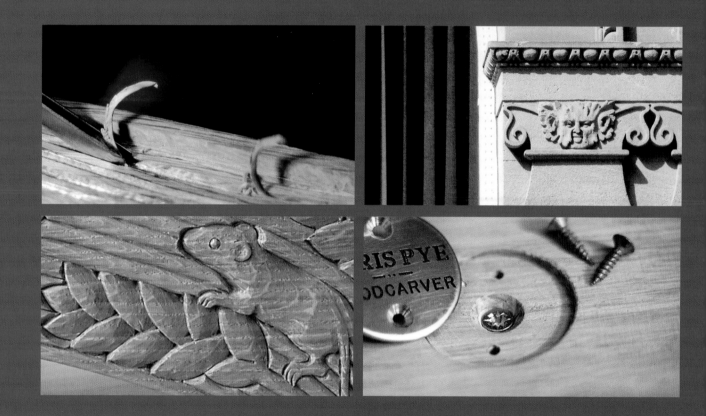

Part Five
Simple Projects

- Off the Books

- Take a Bow

- Architectural Inspiration

- Door Mouse

- Memento

Off the Books

This commemorative carved book has many possibilities for a variety of ornamental work. The basic shape will inspire carvers to create their own inscriptions.

▲ Above: A relief carved letter B by Deborah Hurst.

◄ Above left: A book, to be acutely studied with notepad and sketchbook.

I was recently approached by a charity to carve them a wooden commemorative 'book'. The carving was to display a photograph and brass inscription plate that remembered the late, and much missed, president. The charity had already had someone attempt the project but were disappointed with the result. The inscription plate and the photograph would be pinned so the pages had to be plain and smooth.

In this chapter I am going to show you how to carve the basic book in the hope that you might choose to take it further – such as lettering the inscription rather than having a brass plate for example. Another idea that would work in this context is including a carved ornamental letter, such as the 'B' shown in the photo above.

The wood

I started with a block of warmly coloured English oak (*Quercus robur*), measuring 18⅜ x 10⅜ x 1½in (470 x 265 x 38mm) and planed all around. Using oak was a personal choice and any interesting hardwood will suffice. You could also 'bookmatch' the wood split and join the wood down the centre so the figure of one 'page' is matched on the other. If you are incising letters or carving the page surfaces, be wary of too much figure as this may obscure or camouflage the shadows of your work. Run the grain across the width of the book (in the direction of writing). This is important because you need maximum strength at the ends of the spine, where the carving is thin and most vulnerable. I held my block gripped to the bench with clamps or fences of wood when working on the page surfaces and in an ordinary bench vice when carving the ends of the spine.

Design

Starting at the beginning, the most important thing to understand is perhaps the most obvious – this is not a book but a woodcarving. It only has to look like a book. So as an essential preparation exercise, carefully observe books as objects and make decisions on which forms and shapes are important, and which can be simplified. Above all, you want a convincing first impression. If you look carefully at a book lying open you will notice several things. These include:

■ The pages separate into 'folios' – clumps rather than individual sheets.

■ The ends of the pages above the spine form an interesting, pyramid-shaped hole.

■ There is a little gap beneath the point at which the cover and spine meet and the tabletop.

■ The cover is distinct, both in colour and material.

■ These are the sorts of things to note and sketch down – they are what makes a book recognizable as a book.

Template

Make an accurate template of one half of one end of the book see drawing below and overleaf. The template should include the spine itself, the curve of the page surface and the lie of the cover. It's worth taking your time over this since all other shaping and carving follows from it **1**. As a book is not only symmetrical but each end is the same, the template can be used for all the marking out; repeating or flipping it over from a centre line (representing the crease in the middle) as appropriate.

1 Marking out the ends with a template.

2 Shaping the page surfaces. You can see the cover has been separated from the pages, and the steps made when I removed waste wood with my tablesaw and router.

The template, made from stiff thin cardboard or plastic, must include all the important information. This template will guide all shaping and carving decisions.

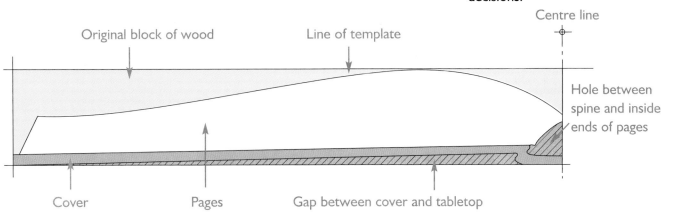

Original block of wood

Line of template

Centre line

Hole between spine and inside ends of pages

Cover

Pages

Gap between cover and tabletop

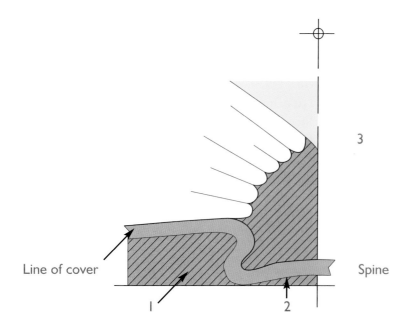

3

Line of cover

Spine

1   2

Close up of the spine, a tight 'S' bend.

The gap between the cover and table (1) and the arch of the spine (2) only go deep enough to create the illusion. Note the line of the pages extends beyond the cover and into the space above the spine (3).

Rough separation of cover and pages

Using the template as your guide with regard to depth, start the work by removing wood around the block with the tablesaw, so recessing the pages from the cover **2**.

When a book is open, note that at the sides the cover lies on the table while at the ends it rises up and away from the table to its junction with the spine. This means that you must remove a different amount of wood from the ends compared to the sides. In my case the saw cut left ¼in (6mm) at the sides, but a full 1in (25mm) at the top and bottom.

Page surfaces

I took wood away from the crease between the pages with a narrow cutter in my router, cut-by-cut. I then used it to produce the curve on the pages themselves. The template is invaluable here – the sequential cuts from the router must stop short of the line you have drawn. If careful, the subsequent smoothing work is more a matter of removing the corners of the cuts and merging the whole together.

After the machining, clean up with a wide, flat gouge and spokeshave. Make sure you get smooth and flowing surfaces, losing the flat top surface of the original block. Keep looking at the end profile of the pages. Ignore the line of the template, it only serves as a guide. Lift the outer edge of the pages up so you have a lovely S-shaped curve.

A drum sander is the best tool for finishing the concave outer sections of the pages. Carve deep and sharp into the centre crease in the middle of the book, without going too deep at the far ends **3**. Finish the pages by sanding, dampening and smoothing further.

Tools

A router will make light work of removing the initial waste in a neat and uniform way. If you don't have one, you will have to go the long way round with gouges and chisels. A spokeshave and drum sander speed up the shaping and smoothing of the pages. Only the ends of the spine require proper carving tools.

The outside of the cover and spine

When the book is resting open on the table, the cover only touches at the outer edges. There is a little shadow either side of the spine as the cover rises away from the table to join it. Mark this clearly with the template for tackling next.

Cut back the line of the cover about ½in (12.5mm). This is all that is needed to give the effect. Remember that this book is not designed to be picked up and turned over, but 'lie' open, displaying the photo and plaque. You could, however, choose to carve a full spine if you wanted the carving to be handled.

Scribe a line on the back of the block, nibble away waste with a deep gouge and clean up with a chisel. Shape the junction of the spine with the cover **4**. A V tool is ideal for cleaning up here. Lastly on the outside, shape the spine itself. This is slightly arched and carving this adds a touch of panache **5**.

Inside of cover and spine

Using the template as a guide, remove wood from the inside line of the cover by nibbling away waste with a deep gouge and cleaning up with a chisel **6** and **7**. Try not to cut into the pages themselves and make sure you leave the cover a uniform thickness – in my case this was ⅛in (3mm). You will find that you'll need small gouges for the inside folds of the spine **8**. Do not cut the hole at the moment. When you have finished the spine check the run of the cover edge around the book, corner to corner and across the spine.

End hole of spine

If there is an esoteric bookbinder's term for the hole between the spine and the inner ends of the pages which appears when the book is flexed open, I'm unaware of it. Excavating this hole is the trickiest bit of the carving. Getting the depth and shape right is essential.

The most important question is 'how deep should you carve?' The general rule is 'deep enough to do the job' but not too deep, as this will significantly weaken the carving. In my case ½in (12.5mm) was enough. As for the shape, I have found that a sort of 'cave' works best, being deeper at the base (against the spine) and curving down from the crease in the pages above. Effectively, you are making a deep undercut. The viewer looks down on the book and all we need is an illusion that the hole goes right the way through. This shape also stops the deep cut that is the crease between the pages from penetrating the roof of the hole. Before you begin cutting the peculiar shape of the hole, note the slight curve to the walls and the way the inner ends of the pages are staggered

3 For the page fold I swapped from spokeshave to flat gouges. Do not go too deep at the top and bottom and penetrate the roof of the hole above the spine at the end.

4 Turn the block over and cut back the slope of the cover.

5 The spine itself has a lovely little curve – another touch that makes the book 'read' true.

against the cover. Draw the lines limiting the hole carefully. Pick a gouge to set in the curved wall of the hole, symmetrically on both sides **10**. Bore out the middle of the waste wood first **11** and then clean up with a selection of gouges **12**. Don't lever against the spine! If you have a Dremel or a similar type of multi-tool it will help you to clean up the bottom of the hole.

Separating pages

You have now created a convincing cover and all that remains is to separate the pages in their block. It is best to treat the pages as 'folios' or clumps, as opposed to individual sheets, which might detract from the impression for which we are aiming. For the top and bottom, I used a 45° V tool, but a narrow U gouge (veiner) will suffice **13**.

Draw out the lines first. Don't make them too parallel as a little variation adds interest. Join the tops and bottoms together at the sides. I used a 'scratch stock' to run these grooves, a simple L-shaped tool made from scrap wood and an old hacksaw blade **14**.

Finish the ends of the folios at the spine by rounding between the ends of the grooves **15**. You have now finished the book, unless of course you wish to letter the pages.

6 Nibbling back the waste with a deep gouge.

7 Cleaning up the inside line of the cover with a flat chisel.

8 A small gouge cuts the inside folds of the spine.

9 Finished spine. At this point the edge cover should run in a continuous, smooth and logical line around the book.

10 Stabbing in the curved inner ends of the pages gives a neat scored line to work up to.

11 Boring out the waste – take great care not to foul the spine.

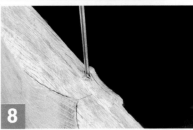

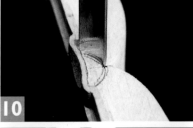

Finishing

I slightly stained the cover of the carving, adding a lot of realism, and gave the whole piece a quick wax polish to bring out the lovely grain. If you were going to carve letters into the surface of the pages, you would be looking for a mild amount of figuring or pattern so as not to camouflage your work. If the pages serve to 'frame' a picture, as here, then the more interesting the figuring the better.

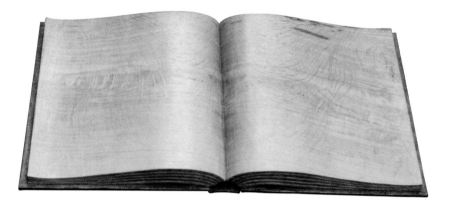

▲ Finished book after staining of the cover and waxing, but before applying the brass and photograph.

▲ The finished book with brass inscription plate pinned to the left page and brass-framed photograph on the right. There is a lot more that could be done with this basic carving.

12 Cleaning up the junctions inside of the hole with a veiner.

13 Separating folios with a 45° V tool.

14 The straight side edges of the pages are cut with a scratch stock. Hidden and running along behind the cover, I am holding the leg of the L-shaped stock from which the position of the scratch is taken.

15 The finished book before staining.

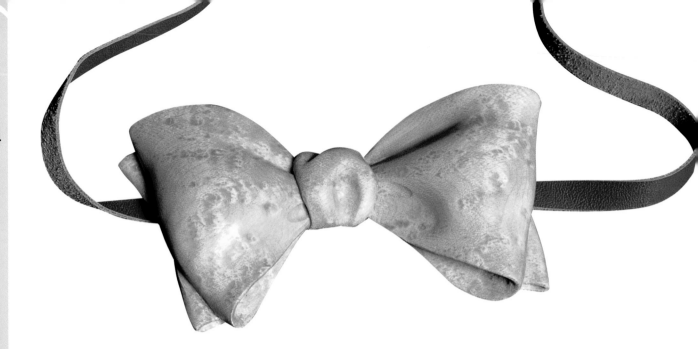

Take a Bow

If, in an informal setting, bow ties generally indicate a somewhat eccentric, colourful personality, what can one say about someone wearing a wooden one?

▲ The finished bow tie in bird's-eye maple.

Design

Bow ties come in a huge variety of shapes, from the black, tight, ready-folded ones of the wedding reception, to the flamboyant works of art sported by some of our more colourful television presenters. There's a lot of choice in the type of bow tie you can carve and before you can reach any concrete decision you will need to research them █.

To make your bow tie 'read' correctly, you need to consider the following:
█ How the knot compresses the wings so that the more complicated folds are nearer the centre, from which they fan out.
█ The fabric, which needs to be smoother, rounder and under less tension towards the outside edge.
█ Gravity, which unless you are making a stiff and formal ready-made bow tie, will have some effect on the hang of the material furthest away from the knot.

Steer clear of symmetry but keep a balance on both sides. Find ways of making the silhouette interesting – one side of the bow could be slightly larger than the other, for example. Pay attention to making the knot attractive, but bear in mind what neck loop fixing will lie behind it. The knot of the bow tie lies around the top button of your shirt. We all have different shirts and neck sizes! By overlaying drawings of possible bow ties on an actual-size digital print (or measured drawing) of your own preferred shirt collar, you will position the knot correctly and get the most effective size and shape of the bow.

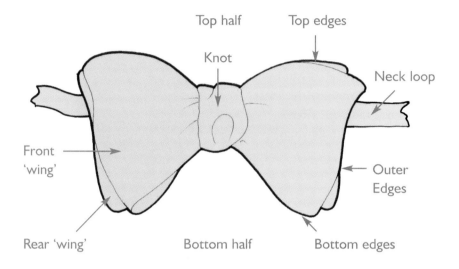

Thickness: 1in (25mm)

Making models

Despite all my drawing, the one thing I was unsure of was the thickness of my carving. Wood is heavier than cloth, and too thick a bow tie will hang awkwardly and probably be uncomfortable. So I made a model in clay, and would advise you to do the same 2 .

Your model doesn't have to be complete in every detail although it should be actual size. After all, its objective is to provide you with more information. Your photos and drawings are two-dimensional but your model is three-dimensional, which will help you solve several basic design questions. These include:

- Where the masses lie.
- Whether the top half should be thicker than the bottom.
- How much of the rear 'wing' you should show.
- How the outer edges round over to show the fold of the material that makes the actual bow.
- How much of the top and bottom edges will be seen when you wear it.
- How deep you should undercut the hollows where the edges of the fold show.
- The minimum thickness needed to create the illusion of fullness.

It's a bit like an interrogation and I wouldn't hesitate to say the design stages are more important than the carving itself which is relatively simple. The more you can pin down now, the easier you will arrive at

1 My research entailed looking at sketches, photographs and, of course, a real bow tie.

2 The best sense of the bow tie's three dimensions will come from a simple model in clay or plasticine.

your bow tie. It could well take you longer to prepare like this than to do the actual carving, but this is the professional approach and the one most likely to ensure good results. Follow your design in this method and you will get a great-looking bow tie, even if your technique is a little rough. You don't want to find problems while you go along as by then it will often be too late to put them right. There will still be room for subtleties in the carving but get the big decisions nailed before you lay on with your chisel. And, while you are at it, consider how the thickness and creases in the knot affect how you fix the neck loop on? Create a full-size working drawing from your research, model and drawings.

Wood

As always your choice of wood is vital to the success of the carving. This is not a bow tie but a piece of wood and it could be argued that if you want to wear something that looks exactly like a bow tie, wear a real one.

You may think you should choose a timber with a strong pattern or figure, but I would advise against this. In a real bow tie, the pattern of the material will naturally run up and down the 'hills and valleys' as it is folded. Cutting the bow tie out of a block of wood means that stripy figuring will simply sweep across the form willy-nilly in an unnatural way. Joining the wood so the wings of the tie 'book match' across the central knot might get around this although it will add a lot to the work.

If you choose too strong a figure, the pattern will simply camouflage the form of the bow tie. The 'form' – and by this we mean the flow and arrangement of masses – is a very lovely thing in a bow tie and worth making the most of. So the blander the wood, the more the form is revealed simply and elegantly. Having said that there is, of course, a limit to the amount of blandness you want.

We need to strike a balance between some interest in the figure, and letting the form run free. A burr would be ideal. I was lucky enough to have a piece of bird's-eye maple (*Acer saccharum*) which admittedly isn't the nicest wood to carve but has the perfect subtlety of figure with small nacreous spots. Run the grain across the bow tie for maximum strength. Wood is of course much heavier than cloth and we will reduce the weight of the finished carving by hollowing out the back of the wings just before we fix the neck loop.

Preparation

Transfer your working drawing to the wood and cut out the profile of the bow tie with a bandsaw, scrollsaw or coping saw. Both sides of the wood should of course be planed beforehand. You will need to carve all over and around the workpiece so too many clamps will get in the way. Glue and clamp your blank to a board (which you can clamp in turn to your bench) using thick paper in between. Dilute your PVA to make releasing the carving easier **3**. You now have your drawings, photos and model nearby, your bow-tie blank clamped securely and your sharp carving tools to hand.

The carving

General shaping

Before you start, pause and think about what you are trying to do. Try to see the shape in the wood. Mark the high spots on the carving, where the wood remains at maximum thickness. The first cut should be across each end of the knot, a job ideal for a saw. This will allow the first bulky waste wood to fall away more easily **4**. Your first stage is 'bosting in' – roughing the wood to shape and getting a feel of the whole thing. Don't worry about detail or smaller elements at this point. Work down from the high spots towards the knot, which will end up less deep than the wings **5**.

Remember that as you remove wood it is that which remains that is your carving. Keep the feeling of fullness and roundness, remembering that only the back of the carving should be flat. The rest should flow and sweep around. You might find that drawing a centre line helps keep a sense of balance and proportion. Don't be in a hurry, try and let the form develop naturally. You should find the front and rear wings 'naturally' separate. Keep the bow tie simple, with some plain surfaces to allow the figure of the wood to show.

Refinement

Once the main shape is in, you can turn to refining what you've got. Firstly, firm up the knot, remembering that the material for the bow on any side arises from it. In other words, the knot wraps around (outside) the inner edge of the bows, compressing them.

Secondly, as you come around the shape, just follow it underneath so that you are not so much deliberately undercutting as allowing the undercutting to arise from the form. At each outer edge separate the rounded fold of the front wing from the rear wing behind it and set it in. The next step is to divide the top and bottom edges of the front and rear wings so they are distinct from each other. The rear wings need only be about ⅛in (3–4mm) thick but will show the edges of the fabric coming together **6**.

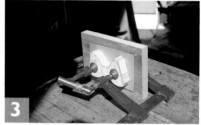

3 The bandsawn wooden blank clamped in a 'glue and paper sandwich'.

4 A calculated saw cut across the ends of the knot at the beginning helps with subsequent chopping away of the initial waste wood.

5 Roughing out the main forms.

6 Modelling – getting in the folds of the bow at the top and bottom edges.

You should see your bow tie coming into shape now as you refine and consolidate the various elements. Besides carving tools, you may find a burr cutter on something like a Dremmel useful in the tight hollows near the knot.

If the holding board is hindering your carving, take it to the bandsaw and cut away what excess you can. It may mean screwing the remaining board to the bench or switching to a carver's screw. To finish off the surface, switch from carving tools to scrapers (with an intermediate stage of rifflers if necessary). I make these by grinding and chamfering the ends of old hacksaw blades. Take the trouble to keep the wood surface clean from now on **7**.

From scraping, turn to sanding. You should be able to start with 150 grit. I worked through grades to a final 360 grit, damping and letting dry in between **8**. Finish the front of the bow tie, and as far around the sides and edges as you can. There are likely to be points you can't reach comfortably because of the holding board, even if it is cut away. Remove the carving from the backboard with a spatula inserted along the sandwiched paper. Clean off the paper remaining on the back of the carving by rubbing it on flat sandpaper.

There are two remaining carving jobs to be done – cleaning up the edges and hollowing the wings. Now you have taken the carving off its support, the trickiest thing will be holding it safely as you work.

Carving the edges

The edges of the bow tie will be visible from the side when you wear it. To give the best illusion of a real tie, you need to clean up all around and define the front and rear bows clearly. I found the best grip for the carving was across the bows, in my carver chops. An ordinary bench vice will do although the advantage of the chops is their greater working height and accessibility **9**.

Hollowing out the wings

Now turn to the back of the carving. You will notice a lot of surplus wood behind each bow and you will need to remove as much of this as you can, while retaining the strength. You should be able to reduce the weight by at least a third **10**.

I found the best place to grip the bow tie was across the knot, but your approach may be different because of the shape. You will need to take it easy as the knot/bow junction is one of the carving's weak points. Examine each bow carefully and mark out the area from where you will remove surplus wood. Take out the wood with short bent spoon gouges and scrapers, or high-speed burrs, using your finger and thumb as a guide to the remaining wood thickness. Finish off neatly – friends will want to look at the back! You may want to sign your name somewhere in the hollow at this point. I used a pyrograph.

7 After smoothing as best you can with carving tools, turn to scrapers to further flatten and refine the surface.

8 From scraping turn to sanding. Finish off as much of the visible part of the bow tie as you can before removing from the holding board.

Fitting the neck loop

A bought bow tie is very lightweight and has an even lighter attaching ribbon. Being considerably heavier, our wooden version needs something a little thicker to prevent the tie sagging as we wear it. I used a ⅜in (9mm) wide strip of thin leather across the knot, held by a recessed washer. The leather strip itself was recessed further **11**. Take great care not to pass any screws through the knot and out the front! The ends of the loop, which you pass around your neck, can be tied together, or fitted with an adjustable hook and eye. You could alternatively use Velcro.

Finishing

It would have been easy to bruise or damage the sanded front surface of your bow tie in the preceding stages, so do check it over in a different light for blemishes and repair them before applying a finish. You will need a simple finish to bring out the grain of your wood, something like Danish oil and beeswax. I used white shellac on my bird's-eye maple, which kept the wood a pale blonde colour while emphasizing the eyes.

9 Once the carving is off the backing board, begin to clean up the edges.

10 I have marked the areas at the back of the bows where wood can be safely removed to lighten the carving.

11 Detail of the neck loop attachment. There must be many ways of fixing it and whichever you choose, plan carefully.

◄ The final carving.

Architectural Inspiration

The façades of Victorian and Edwardian buildings can offer rich pickings for recreating architectural designs. Keeping an observational eye when walking through towns and cities can offer great inspiration.

Woodcarvers often want carvings to copy – good examples that they can study and use for practice. Well, there is a frequently overlooked source: the façades of Victorian and Edwardian buildings. The stonework outside buildings from this period is rich in mouldings and architectural detail, festoons of flowers, mythological beasts and idealized human faces.

Stonecarving is not the same as woodcarving; the tools, techniques and materials used in the process are quite different. Nevertheless, stonecarving, by the very nature of being a 'glyptic' (reductive) process, is a lot closer to woodcarving than modelling, and is usually more easily adapted, and certainly repays close inspection by us woodcarvers.

Research

Binoculars are very helpful – sometimes you are looking at quite a height – and there will be a 'best' time of day, when the light produces the most useful, descriptive shadows. When you find some stone detail worth capturing, return with your camera, take photographs and make notes in a sketchbook. With digital cameras and computer software you can crop, enlarge and print to a size from which you can make working drawings. Unfortunately, without a telephoto lens, you may have to work from a small print.

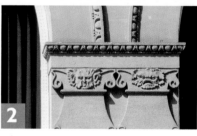

1 Clare Street, Bristol, a wealth of architectural detail. Just above the white walls at ground level, and on either side of the windows, are pilasters (rectangular columns projecting from the wall) atop of which are small relief faces.

2 Two of the faces easily missed as you pass below: a green man and a sort of classic dolphin head with teeth.

Remember that carvings, especially those in lime and other soft stones, may well be worn, or their detail lost in shadow, and you have to sympathetically invent. It's also best not to think of just copying what you see, rather, use what you find to learn from, and go with your own inclination and sense of design.

Basic project

Here we have an example to illustrate the point  and ; a typical ornate Victorian building, quite possibly a bank at some time, and easy to walk past. Look up a little and there, looking back down, are a series of foliate and grotesque faces, carved in chunky relief **3** . Any one of these faces would make an ideal basic project **5** – **9** , but for now, I have chosen one that was a bit unusual, a sort of Greek or Roman dolphin with a tongue **4** .

Preparation

Having scanned in my photo, I enlarged and printed it. From this print, I made my working drawing with tracing paper, adjusting and adding various elements that were unclear. A centre line will help keep the carving symmetrical. Always consider the grain direction – this is stone, not wood, and there may be unexpected weak points where the fibres are short. I next transferred the drawing to my wood, English Oak, with tracing paper **10**.

My carving was 10½in (270mm) wide, 6½in (315mm) high and ½in (12.5mm) thick. I decided to do away with the background altogether by band- and scrollsawing neatly around the subject. If you do not have access to these machines, use a coping saw instead.

To hold the wood for carving, I glued the workpiece to a waste piece of plywood with thick paper in between – the so-called 'paper sandwich' method that allows you to get all around the carving without clamps getting in the way. A carver's screw would also be a good alternative.

Carving

There are little holes towards the edges of the face where the acanthus-like leaves overlap. These holes force a certain flow to the design and can be usefully bored early on **11**. The carving here is relatively straightforward but before you start, look at the natural lines of the face and the bony masses, how they have been directed and turned into foliage. Look for heavy shadows – such as between the eyes and mouth – signifying depth, and decide what must be high spots – such as the fish

3 Side view of one relief: chunky and not undercut at all, to keep the strength in the stonework.

4 The carving I chose for this article – a sort of Greek or Roman dolphin with tongue.

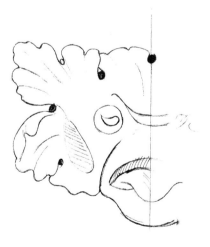

5–9 Any one of these faces would make an interesting practice carving.

eyes, upper lip, cheek bones and tip of tongue. A good plan with a symmetrical carving like this, is to work on one side for a while, which will mean carving away your reference lines drawn on the surface **12**. After a while, redraw this half from the second half, as yet untouched.

Carve the second half for a while, in turn carving away your lines, then redraw from the first half. In this way, you can go back and forth between sides and keep a uniformity of appearance with the centre line as reference. Work from the high spots in, looking to shape the principal masses and flow of the piece, gradually deepening and strengthening your carving – what carvers call 'bosting in' **13**.

Remember, you are trying to feel what the original carver did and not simply copy. You can allow yourself a certain amount of artistic freedom, particularly when you lose the drawing entirely. Rather than just hollow around the tongue, shape the tongue itself, back and inside the mouth, and let the space around take care of itself **14**.

Round over the eyeballs like marbles and cut-in the U-shaped pupils – one of the features of this classic fish face **15**. Take the leaves smoothly to the edge, keeping the surfaces smooth and flowing **16**. Allow the edges to be slab-like, ending in a wall about a quarter of the way from the bottom.

Finishing

Once surfaces and junctions have been cleaned up, simply wax the carving with several thin coats of beeswax, brushed in while warming the wood with a hair dryer. To remove the carving, slide a metal spatula or thin knife along the paper between the work and the supporting plywood, and the face should simply lift away **17**.

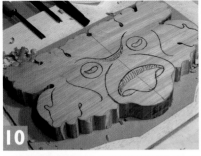

10 Ready to start, with the subject drawn, the work piece cut out and glued down, and the acanthus 'eyes' bored out.

11 Carving one side of the face first using drawn lines on the opposite side for reference.

12 Copying onto the second side what has been carved onto the first.

13 You can gradually deepen the carving as you begin to feel your way into the forms.

14 Carve the tongue into the mouth and then take care of the surrounding space. In this way, the tongue remains large and strong. If you tackle the space around first, it tends to get bigger and the tongue whittled away.

15 For the pupils, make holes at each end by rotating small, quick gouges, and cut an arc in between with a larger tool.

16 Finish off the leaves simply and boldly, letting them flow naturally and smoothly.

17 Once you have lifted the carving away from the supporting ply, clean up the visible edges. You can see here that nothing is undercut.

Door Mouse

This attractive project depicting a harvest mouse and an owl carved into an arch is designed to add a decorative touch to a doorway.

▲ The finished arch in oak on the workbench, width 36in (920mm) and height 7in (180mm).

I made this simple arch for a local client who lives in an old, oak-beamed farmhouse. The arch was to replace a dull, false lintel and generally bring a decorative element to the doorway of a hall corridor. It is designed to be discretely screwed into position with oak pegs hiding the fixings.

Apart from the interesting design, the fascinating part for me was being able to use my 'scratch stock', something that I rarely get to use. I was reminded how versatile this old-fashioned and simple tool is, given the right job – and this was certainly a situation in which it would have been impossible to substitute a router.

Design

The client more or less had the design in mind at the start, reflecting his love of the local countryside: a harvest mouse among the corn, with its tail characteristically curled around a stem and, in the centre, an owl. All I needed to do was join the ideas together and adapt the elements to carving in wood.

'Adapting' in this instance meant 'stylization' – but what exactly does that mean? Essentially, as carvers we stylize a subject when we change how it looks from 'real' to 'carved'. In other words, the manner in which we make it and the tools we use influence its appearance and result. In the same way, cartoonists 'stylize' politicians when they depict them with a pen or brush, or sculptors allow the way they worked the clay to show in a portrait.

There are two reasons for stylizing. Firstly, as the maker, it's frankly easier and more efficient: we work with the carving tools, letting them create and imply, say, a 'mouse'. It's far more difficult to render something absolutely real anyway – as all wildlife carvers know. And efficiency has to do with cost, with the client's budget.

Secondly, in this context, the viewer is never going to be fooled into thinking the mouse in the brown oak arch is really a mouse, any more than thinking a boat in a painting is really a boat. So there is no point attempting to carve reality here anyway. Nonetheless, the carving must tell the viewer everything which they need to know in order to read 'mouse' and, in its own way, be both interesting and beautiful.

Type of carving

The type of carving the client wanted is what is known as intaglio (pronounced with a silent 'g': 'in-tally-o'), where the design is carved straight into the wood without the background being taken away. Normally, the original surface is simply left alone, but in this case, I filled it in with ears of corn. If you put a straight edge over the finished carv-ing, the virtual plane of the original surface is quite evident. I think the final carving would have been the stronger for having the mice and ears of corn proud, either by cutting from the block or glued on as blocks, but clients and budgets rule.

Scratch stock

I cut out and finished the arch, allowing for a little wood where the tail of the owl protruded, and then put a little bead moulding on the corners with my scratch stock **1**. At this point, I transferred my working drawing **2** to the wood with carbon paper.

1 Working the bead moulding on the edges. Keep the scratch stock 'fence' firmly against the side of the wood and work light strokes forward and backward to begin with until you find the right direction for the grain, then gradually deepen your cut by drawing or pulling.

2 I transferred the working drawing to wood with trusty carbon paper, four times in all, on both sides and reversing each end. I needed to adjust this drawing later to take into account the truer run of the stems as they arose from the work of the scratch stock.

The scratch stock  is an effective, low-tech way of moulding edges and, in this case, the stems of corn throughout. It's easy to make: two L-shaped pieces of wood that screw together, and clamp a thin blade bearing the required profile. I use old hacksaw blades for the cutters, ground crisp and square into a sharp cutting profile.

The method is definitely scraping, not cutting, and you have to be careful not to tear the fibres of the wood by 'scratching' against the grain, but with careful handling, the scratch stock can be very successful in creating beads, and surprisingly large moulding profiles.

With the 'fence' against the curved arch, I incrementally defined and shaped the lines of stems that stream between the islands of corn ears **4** by adjusting the position of the blade in the scratch stock. To make sure I was consistent, I worked the same blade position on all four corners of the design before changing it.

I had to go over a few of the stems with my carving tools, tidying, adjusting and deepening the groove in between, but overall I was very pleased at how well the scratch stock performed – almost like ploughing. I led the stems into the areas where I intended carving the mice and corn ears, and finely sanded their surfaces to finish **5**.

I found I had to adjust my drawings of mice and corn ears to take into account the new lines driven by the scratch stock, cleaning off the wood surface with a scraper before redrawing them. In particular, I needed the edges of the ears of corn to line up along grooves in between stems with each ear of corn spanning five stems. This would make the next stage of carving easier, and give a cleaner and stronger appearance to the subject.

3 The scratch stock with protruding blade and alternative cutters, made from old hacksaw blades. You set the amount the cutting edge protrudes, and its distance from the right-angled leg or 'fence'.

4 The scratch stock created a river of stems, accurately relating to the inside edge of the arch – much neater than my drawings.

5 Scratching in and finely finishing the stems was a long and tedious job. Here I am ready to start carving the ears of corn.

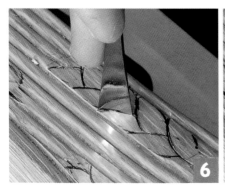  

Corn

I now turned to the ears of corn. The essential 'chip carving' nature of how I carved these ears is shown in the sequence of photographs **6**–**10**. In intaglio carving, you need to make the outline of the subject strong in order to tell the viewer immediately what they are looking at.

The work here is a perfect example of stylization – the gouges create the corn quickly and easily. The resulting 'corn' pales compared to the real thing but cannot be anything else. The trick is to pick the gouges to create the outlines straight away. Fishtails are best, since you need to sink the corner in between the ears. You'll find an inside bevel a great help in working upside down. You can also model the grain a little, as if it were a normal relief carving.

6 Start by picking a flattish gouge for the inside of each grain of corn and stabbing in vertically. Go deeper into the junction between the grains. It is here we want to leave a deep shadow.

7 Switch to deeper gouge for the outside of the grains, and stab in similar fashion.

8 Reverse the gouge to round over the grain.

9 Swinging the cutting edge round while pushing the corner right down into the junction, removing a deep chip.

10 Use a small skew chisel to clean up the recesses. I deepened these back later with a triangular pointed punch.

Mice

The harvest mice represented the only scope for variation in this carving, and whilst making sure I depicted those features that characterize the animal, I did want to give them a little individuality **11 12**.

I started the carving with the same idea as the corn: a strong outline within which to model the subject. I picked appropriate gouges to set in vertically around the edge of the drawing **13** then brought in and finished off the stems up to this outline trench.

The trickiest bit of carving were the tails of the mice, which wrap around the stems **11** otherwise it was a straightforward piece of carving, modelling within the outline. I tried to get as much depth and shadow as I could to prevent the carving looking flat. At the end of the day, intaglio is a light carving, near the surface, and we must make the most of what we have.

11 One of the two left corner mice. The tail wraps around a stem; very characteristic of harvest mice. I'm trying to get as much depth as possible, 'tilting' the mouse to give a more interesting perspective.

12 One of the two mice on the right. Still some cleaning up to do in the junctions and recesses.

13 The principle of intaglio carving is the same: create a strong outline, and then model the subject within it. Here the outline runs into the stems of corn themselves.

Lion's feet

Three chunky lion's feet extended the width of the base to increase stability **4**. For the feet I made a model in clay. This helped me to fit the feet to the curve of the lowest plate and speeded up the carving, enabling me to profile accurately on the bandsaw and take measurements etc. The feet were simply bolted on, with the 'heels' of the paws passing under the edge of the base to take the weight.

The stem

The trickiest part of making the stem was boring the axial hole to take the studding. I needed a 24in (610mm) bit, my lathe, and a lot of patience – working from each end in turn. The hole ends were plugged and the block turned to shape, with a spigot at each end to lock into base and eagle. The carving derived from what I could see in the original photo.

The gothic 'ball flowers' were fun. These have to be made separately as there is no way – or rather, it would take too long – to carve a neat cove behind the flower **5**. The cove I had turned into the stem, using a marble as a profile for the ball flowers. The flowers themselves looked liked lollipops after turning as the balls have spigots beneath which fit into matching, indexed holes around the cove.

The flowers were carved to shape and glued into their holes. The frieze of flowers looks complicated but is really only a repeated pattern of basic tool cuts. If you can carve one square successfully you can carve them all, and in this case the pattern is like a moulding. It's the accurate marking out which counts **6**. I created deeper shadows by punching back the recesses between cuts where possible.

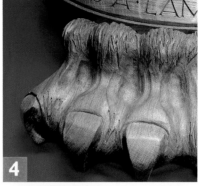

4 Close-up of a lion's foot, fitting into the curve of the lowest base plate. The plate is lettered in Versal with 'Your Word is a Lamp to my Feet'. Note how the vulnerable claws are tucked in to prevent being kicked.

5 Close-up of 'ball flowers' – turned and carved separately. A spigot is inserted into a hole in the turned cove.

Eagle preparation

Because eagle lecterns are designed to carry a Bible they are usually stylized for a flat back. Traditionally they stand on a dome. The eagle was by far the most difficult part of the lectern to design: size, angle, relation to stem axis, jointing, carving the feet and claws from the block to leave a convincing dome all had to be considered. The dome – actually a cylinder – had to align and fit into the stem .

After looking at many eagles I had such a good idea of the bird I wanted to carve that I could work out an accurate drawing to scale without recourse to a model. But I could only relax when I had a block of wood in front of me and could see the eagle was in there waiting to be revealed.

Turning the eagle block upside down and using a jig for accuracy, I bored the hole to take the end of my threaded bar. This hole differed from the one passing axially through the stem and base in that it was narrow enough for me to force the bar to cut its own thread in the wood. In other words, the eagle acted as a great big nut at the top end of the bar, and I eventually fixed it permanently with two-part resin-based glue.

The other, lower, end of the threaded bar emerged from below the base, and a conventional nut pulled and locked the whole together. Using the peg in this hole as a pivot, as before, I routed around the bottom 1in (25mm) of the dome to create a neat cylinder. This part critically fitted the stem and gave me a reference point for carving the semicircular dome between the eagle's feet which in this instance were fairly small in the original. Although I had *some* licence, I still had to make this sort of reference to the original where possible.

6 Frieze of flowers breaks into repeated squares turned 45° to a diamond position. The carving is simple but precise. Extra shadows are created by punching back the spaces between elements.

7 Back view of the dome and eagle's rear claws. Getting the dome to run smoothly around the feet was done by eye.

Blocking up the eagle
5mm = 1in

Body block

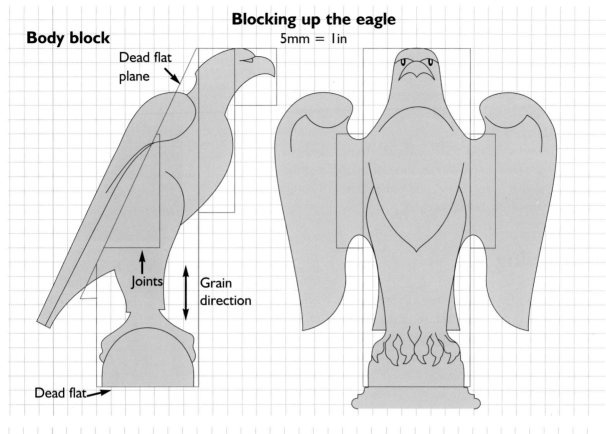

Dead flat plane

Joints

Grain direction

Dead flat

Wings block

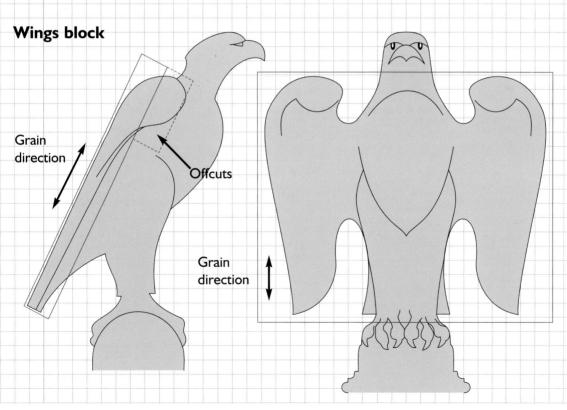

Grain direction

Offcuts

Grain direction

Lastly, with the eagle still upside down, I bolted on a square block to fit my bench vice although, for most of the carving, I held the eagle with a carver's screw, using my adjustable stand **8** Back the right way up, the last part of this block preparation stage was to fit the wings **9**.

The block for the body had vertical grain to provide some strength in the legs, but was sliced at an angle at the back to take the flat board of the wings. Marrying these two surfaces took a long time, necessitating getting right down to the old 'chalk and rub'. To add further stability, I also dowelled the joint in places not affected by the carving – cross-orientation of grain is never ideal – and clamped well. The joint was invisible when over-carved with feathers.

Eagle carving

The carving followed the usual pattern of bosting in, modelling and surface details. I used the Arbortech to create the main forms, losing the corners and blockiness of the original wood **10**. I switched to the slower but more relaxed progress of large gouges to refine the underlying forms, blocking out the legs, feet and head before refining the forms further – but not finishing anything off – consolidating some shapes with rasps and rifflers **11**.

At this stage the bird looked naked – more suitable for the dinner table – but the important work was done; the surface details would now float home in their correct places, starting with the pupil, beak and nostrils, down to a clothing of feathers. The feathers are simple and stylized, drawn out first and relieved from each other. A central vein was run with a tilted V tool, and barbs incised with crescent cuts from a fishtail gouge. All the carving, with the exception of beak and claw, was left from the chisel **12**.

8

9

8 Fixing wood to the inverted eagle block for holding in the vice. Below is the routed cylinder which makes up the lowest part of the dome.

9 Wing board clamped to the back of the eagle block. I cut out recesses to gain purchase for the clamps.

10 Preliminary roughing out with the Arbortech. The eagle is held with a carver's screw on an adjustable stand.

11 Using a small spoon gouge to cut in the eagle's nostrils. Note the scratches to the back of the head where the shape was consolidated and refined with rasps.

12 Every tool cut counts in the vigorous but simple carving out of the feathers.

10

11

12

Finishing

When all the lectern parts were complete, assembled and checked, I applied several coats of thin, hot beeswax with stiff brushes. I included a touch of carnauba wax and gave it a little colour with a proprietary brown antique wax. Thinness and melting helped the wax penetrate the wood, and the thinness also prevented clogging in the corners. The slight colour evened out any difference in wood tone without giving a stained look, and the carnauba wax hardened the final finish.

The lectern was delivered in its main parts, glued and assembled around the threaded bar, and clamped together with the lower nut. I'm now depending on the church 'flower ladies' to add some patina.

◀ The base is nothing more than a stack of plates. Shown here are the gothic 'ball flowers' which are turned and carved separately and inserted, and gothic tracery and other elements.

▶ Looking at other lecterns, I discovered that these eagles are always serious and most bad tempered. I tried to achieve a suitably grumpy look.

Phoenix Rising

This chapter follows the preparation work necessary and the practical details of how to carve a phoenix arising from its flaming nest.

▲ The finished phoenix, in English oak, 25in (635mm) across, 7in (180mm) deep at its beak – it was left completely untreated in-situ.

The clients who gave me this commission were the owners of a beautiful country house in Herefordshire which had been devastated by a fire. The damage was so bad that the house needed to be more or less completely re-built. I had already carved some corbels, or brackets, to support a hood over the house's big front door, under which was an empty space. The clients decided that this would be an ideal space for a carved phoenix, arising from its flaming nest. It would also serve as a fitting commemoration of the reconstruction.

Design

Nearly all carving design revolves around two factors – lighting and position. Below the front door was a steep flight of stone steps. The camera angle in **1** is more or less that at which a visitor would see the finished carving, being unable to step further back because of a wall. The head of the phoenix had to clear a thick, arching moulding in the available space behind.

I could see straight away that the viewing distance, angle and shading of the hood meant that whatever I did would have to be bold and simple, with strong shadows. The top of the bird would be hidden – so all top edges (the wings and head) need hardly be undercut at all. Conversely, undercutting would need to be the most severe on the lower edges (flames or smoke) as these would be seen from below by the viewer.

Even the simplest carvings involve some preliminary drawing, a quick sketch or doodle at the very least. As this particular piece was going to be complicated, I knew there would be a lot of time spent at this preparatory stage. As carvers we draw because we don't have enough information in our minds to guide our hands. In other words we can't see enough of what we want to carve. If we could, the exercise would be pointless.

A drawing helps us make a better carving. I began by researching phoenixes, making many thumbnail sketches and working these into provisional ideas. Eventually I arrived at a rough working drawing of how my phoenix might appear **2**. In this case, however, a drawing wasn't enough as I still couldn't 'see' the result as clearly as I would have liked. Since I never start a carving until I can see, the only option was a real three-dimensional model.

Clay modelling

The leap to modelling stuns many carvers who think they have enough to do already! To their mind, clay modelling takes longer than drawing and thus extends the time of the whole job, is a different and difficult skill to master and even worse, represents a betrayal of woodcarving. For me though modelling has the same aim as any drawing in that it helps the carver produce a better woodcarving, plain and simple. To be clear, in this context, modelling isn't about copying. Clay models and woodcarvings are different. They entail different tools, involve different processes and are two different mediums entirely. I never advocate making a model and just copying it in wood. You should see it as a part of your creative process, and one that also includes, and can be seen in the same light as, drawing.

For me, sometime around the bosting stage, usually about a third of the way into the carving, I find that I pay less and less attention to the model and have become more absorbed in the carving. The carving has taken over. I then put the model by and might never look at it again until I return it to the mud from whence it came **3**.

1 You can see the low viewing angle as you look up the steps to the front door and the space beneath the canopy where my phoenix would reside. The acanthus corbels and details in the glass above the door were an earlier part of the carving job.

2 After sketches, I drew something like what I had in mind, full size on a mock up panel of the available space before I began my model.

Virtues of making a model

- Pinning down an idea in the first place.
- Exploring how three-dimensional your idea really is.
- Solving problems of grain strength.
- Measuring wood dimensions for gluing up.
- Assessing waste wood for initial roughing out or bandsawing.
- Acting as a reference or aide-memoire.
- Speeding up the work by saving time in the long run.
- Giving the carver confidence in what they are doing.
- Showing the clients very clearly what you have in mind.

Detail

I modelled the phoenix relief full-size on a board that represented the background space where the carving would sit, complete with the moulding which the head and wings must overlap. I positioned this board on my tilting bench at the angle at which the finished bird would finally be seen. I started with larger lumps of clay, smearing them together to build the main masses . I then added smaller pieces to refine the features, moving from fingers to tools when I got to the details. All the time I tried to visualize my subject, thinking 'how will this look, how will it work in wood?'

To prevent the clay slumping with gravity I used 'butterflies' – little crosses of wood tied by wire and stapled to the board. Because of the viewing angle and the moulding behind, the head had to come right forward. I pushed stiff wire armatures down through the clay to strengthen the neck. I wanted a bird with 'attitude', after all it has just done something quite extraordinary **5**. The body mass was biggest at the chest (pride) and sloped back behind the flames and smoke. I made the eyes strong and piercing. The strong movement in the turn of the head and neck made for asymmetrical wings.

In the end, I had modelled some parts in considerable detail, such as the head, neck and body tilt. Other parts didn't say much, either because I already knew what I was going to do, such as the feathers, or because I didn't have a clue, such as the nest and flames. These latter parts were by far the most difficult to work out and I left most of the designing to the wood stage **6**.

I had decided to make the smoke, flames and nest in two layers of wood. Carvers refer to these as 'flats', carved separately and stacked one on top of the other. Flats would save me a lot of time excavating between elements and also help create a clearer, more spacious feel to the flames and smoke.

3 My working model of the phoenix. It was shown to the clients at this stage for approval. Note how the nest and flames were greatly simplified in the final carving.

4 The little crosses tied by wire to staples are 'butterflies'. Clay has no strength and, like me on some mornings, will readily slump with gravity if not propped up.

5 The head. I'm not so much concerned with the details such as feathers, as with the overall form. The head should be the focus of the design.

Transferring to paper

One of the many good reasons for making a clay model is for measuring wood dimensions. I intended gluing up a starting block of wood, not that I had a block that big. If you look at the finished piece the joins are as good as invisible and I knew this would save me a lot of time and materials. The model is three-dimensional but I would need to cut profiles in effectively two-dimensional boards of wood. Here is my technique for getting working drawings with which to cut the wood profiles on the bandsaw. I also used the model to show me where to hide the joints as neatly as possible. This technique can be adapted for fully three-dimensional models besides reliefs, as here. To take a drawing onto glass, transfer it to paper, and then to the wood, you will need to do the following:

- Lay the model flat on its back.
- Support a thick glass plate on blocks a little above the model (and I do mean thick as you will be resting on it).
- Obtain a set-square (preferably a small one), and something that will enable you to draw on the glass, such as a 'chinagraph' pencil.

There is an immediate and very real difficulty when you look through the two-dimensional glass and draw the profile of a three-dimensional object. This is known as parallax which can be defined as the effect whereby the position or direction of an object appears to differ when viewed from different directions (eg through the lens of a camera).

The upshot is that you can only get an accurate drawing if you keep your eye at the same angle relative to the plane of the glass (which will ultimately be the 'paper plane'). This is where the set-square helps – it is impossible to get an accurate profile without it. I sited along the set square and marked the glass exactly at the corner of the square where it met the surface. Because I used a smaller piece than the whole model, I had to shuffle this glass along on the blocks, a section of the model at a time. However, I prefer having the better reach than stretching over a large sheet – but you can choose otherwise. The golden rule is that the glass must not move while you are drawing **7**.

I find it best not to try and draw continuous lines on the glass but small sections and important points such as contours of inner high spots. I then treat these marks like a 'connect the dots' puzzle. This method, if done correctly, is very accurate. Nevertheless, I always check it with a few measurements of a ruler. I would like to add that I'm also quite generous in allowing waste wood beyond the model – the worse thing that could happen is that you have glued up too little material.

6 Some parts of the model are more like 'notes' for carving.

7 Here I am at the workface, sighting carefully down the set-square to the edges of the phoenix, and its internal contours.

Working drawings

To transfer the profile from the glass to paper, I simply put the paper on the glass and shine a light from behind. I then have a working drawing. In my case, with a small piece of glass, I made my drawing on the glass, transferred it to paper, erased the glass drawing, and then moved the glass along to draw the next section. These drawings married well because I took my time to be accurate.

So, from the model, I had an accurate full-sized outline drawing of the whole piece. I measured the depth of the model at certain points and drew some inner profiles for those pieces of wood needed to bulk up the mass in certain places, these being the neck, head, chest and flats. I also made provisional drawings of the flames and smoke but, for now, I was intending to carve only the phoenix itself, adding the flames etc. as flats later. This part of the carving is shown on page 153.

Blocking up

From my clay model I had the outline of the main shape of the phoenix. I had also calculated wood and contours, with depth measurements, for the fatter parts and high spots. From this information I could select and glue up the wood I needed into a starting block. For the carving I used oak (*Quercus spp.*) that was left completely untreated in-situ. The bird is about 25in (635mm) across and 7in (180mm) deep at its beak. By gluing up a block like this you can see how I had already saved myself a lot of the time it would take to remove waste, had I started from a big lump of wood. Not only that but I now have the model to look at to get me going 8 and 9.

The carving

The carving of the phoenix fell into three distinct parts – the bird itself with its feathers, the smoke and flames and finally the nest. The first stage is to bost in. I used a selection of large gouges and my trusty Arbortech. This is probably the most crucial step in any carving. My primary aim was to the reveal or place the underlying forms, the movement of the wings and the turn of the head. In particular I felt I had to get the head right – this was, after all, the focal point of the design.

10 shows a mixture of Arbortech grooves, gouge and rasp marks. I took a bit off, had a look then took another bit off and had another look... you get the idea. The photo also shows excess wood to the left of the phoenix's head – remaining from the original block. When I had taken the wood back around the head and wings I could confidently cut away wood from behind the bird 11. The head stands alone and is effectively framed by the tops of the wings.

8 The glued up block for starting, with lumps of 'high spot wood' (body, head etc.) added to a back profile of the wings.

9 The block in place of the clay model on my tilting bench, held by a carver's screw and ready to go. You can see the wings bulked out at the top, a lump for body, and more for the head.

Neck feathers

Once I was happy with the head and body forms, I started putting in neck feathers  and then on down to feather the body and wings – leaving a untouched area onto which I intended to fix the flats for the flames and nest.

Remember that this carving is to be seen from a distance, high up above a door and below a hood. The feathers had to be bold and simple and, as there are rather a lot of them, easy to carve. Luckily, since this is a woodcarving and not a real bird, effect can come before truth.

When you carve such feathers you have to plan carefully, looking at real birds and thinking about the size and how they are laid out in relation to the body and wings. It is very important not to make carved feathers too even and monotonous, even if they might be quite uniform in the real thing. Vary the size and shape of your gouges a little.

Strategy

I had decided that I would start with the bird (head, body and wings) and leave a block beneath the body for the flames and nest. The long wing feathers would be easy to carve and simply fall to the back of the flames. Additionally, by building out in layers, or 'flats', I could achieve a lot of clear space between the elements while eliminating the time-consuming need to excavate waste wood from deep areas.

So, I had my wood – its outlines culled from the working drawing and its masses blocked up by calculation from the model. The starting block of wood was held at an angle by a large woodcarver's screw to my tilting bench, as I wanted to see it from the same angle a viewer would see the finished carving. To hand I had my clay model, helping me visualize the finished carving, my sketches, drawings and photographs for reference, my carving tools and most importantly of all, a big cup of tea. So, loin-girded, I cracked straight into the bird.

10 All sense of the 'blockiness' of the glue-up has gone. Note that I haven't carved or pierced the bottom part of the wood yet – this remains flat for gluing on the wood for smoke, flames and nest.

11 The Arbortech again, followed by rasps, removing waste wood from around the back. I had to be careful not to remove too much or the neck would have looked scrawny.

12 I created strong feather shapes by taking away the waste between the stabbed outlines with a skew chisel.

woodcarving projects and techniques

Phoenix Rising

Breast feathers

You can imagine that the quantity of the breast feathers in this big bird called for a lot of patience and discipline, and what a carver needs in a case like this is a technique that is simple, effective, and looks good too (see below). My approach was to stab strong outlines first with my mallet, deepening the cuts in the corners. I separated the shapes with a skew chisel – the deeper corner cuts helps the waste fall away. Looking like fish scales when I'd done, I quickly shaped over the surfaces to give a fuller, more fluffed up, 'feather feeling'.

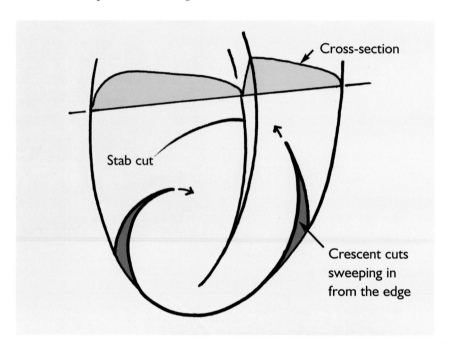

Cross-section

Stab cut

Crescent cuts sweeping in from the edge

A typical feather can be carved with a few effective cuts. Note how the splits cuts curl in from the edges. This is the opposite of carving leaves.

Quills

Then, I made a strong centre quill with angled V tool cuts **13** – this is not so much a real string-like quill form, as a strong shadow. I orientated the quills to give more of a sense of body mass through perspective. Feathers characteristically have splits between barbs and if you show these it makes the feathers read true. Such splits are simply crescent cuts, angled in with different gouges, but they still must be placed carefully, avoiding boring repetition by ringing the changes.

I finished by carving a little twist into their ends. This approach was similar for all the feathers. Carve vigorously and the results are very effective. I finished all the feathers on the bird itself **14** and **15**, leaving the block for the next stage.

Flames and smoke

My master plan was to carve the flames, smoke and nest in at least two layers, or 'flats', overlapping elements and leaving lots of space in between. It's easiest to see more exactly what I mean as we go along. If I hadn't layered the wood like this one of my biggest problems would have been cleaning waste from between each flame and swirl of smoke. By doing so, I saved myself a lot of time and effort later on.

So how on earth does one carve something so ephemeral as flames or smoke? The simple answer is that you can't, not as such. What you have to do is to create the impression – use 'art' and stylization to catch the sense of movement My clay modelling had been a bit unsure at this point. I knew how I was going to proceed, but I had left the flames, smoke and nest a bit vague. I just couldn't get the flames in clay looking as I imagined them in wood – I needed to see my bird in the wood first. And, ultimately, it came down to sheer visualization.

Preparation

So, for me, this meant drawing, drawing and drawing again – more time-consuming hard work. I always bore in mind that I was trying to achieve an effect. I must have done well over 60 separate drawings – cutting, pasting and redrawing until I found what I wanted – a swirling energetic sense of fire and smoke. An impression where the viewer would find it hard to tell the smoke from the flame.

This amount of preparation for a carving sometimes surprises beginners. It may take a long time to get what you want but you have to get it right – after all, your carving may well last longer than you! I had shaped the breast of the bird, finished off the long feathers and left a roughly nest-shaped, flat surface below. I sloped this surface back at about 10°. This angle tilted the layers of smoke and flames forward and away from the wings, giving more sense of space and a better perspective on the flames when viewed from below in their final position.

Trial and error

After a lot of trial and error I had the first flat of the flames and smoke (the inner flat) screwed to the wood left below the body **16**. This too I bevelled so the outer flat of flame and smoke also tilted away. I found the best way to carve each flat or layer of smoke and flame was to cut it out and hold it to a narrow piece of wood with a carver's screw. The wood itself was gripped in my bench vice. This way I could get at all parts of the subject freely, undercut from the back, and carve the flats three-dimensionally **17**.

13 The V tool creating the centre quill. Next, I rounded over the shapes to make them feel fuller, and then cut in the angled, crescent-like splits with suitable fishtail gouges.

14 The bird itself is nearly finished here – I'm hollowing out the wings to take the long feathers.

15 The tips of the wings have been bandsawn. You can see the flat face below the body feathers to which the nest block will be fitted.

The nest

I could have glued on a third flat if necessary to get a bigger nest but, in the many phoenixes that I looked at, the nest was quite small, with the emphasis on the flames and bird. I followed this balance. I had a similar problem here as with the flames – how to get a sense of twigs and sticks that make up the nest.

My solution hinged on the need for the elements to be seen clearly from a distance. I decided to carve an amorphous, 'background' nest and extend the twigs from that by inserting separately carved units 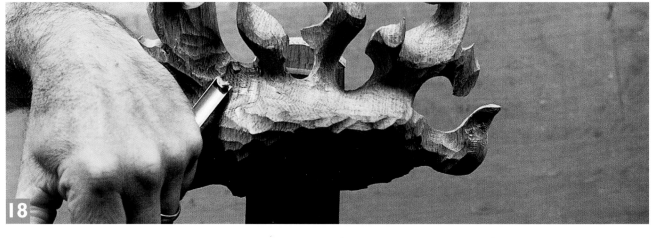. This way I could again save myself what looked like tedious excavating between the twigs. Additionally, I had an answer to the need for grain strength in all those bits sticking out at different angles.

I first gave an overall shape and texture to the lumpy middle part of the second flat with gouges, burrs and cutters with a high-speed flexible shaft. I carved the twigs from thick dowels, which I made myself using a dowel plate from the same wood as the bird. I lined up a 'twig' where I thought it looked good, bored the right-sized hole, and tapped and glued it in. As with the feathers, I was looking for an answer that looked effective but took little effort – I struck gold here and was pleased with the effect.

16 Here is just one of my attempts at flames and smoke. The paper template would be an inner or back layer ('flat'). A second, different arrangement of elements would then be superimposed.

17 The first flat, screwed into position, with a face ready to take the second one.

18 The second flat, held from behind with a carver's screw. Note that the thick lump of wood below the flames will eventually form the nest.

▲ Detail of the resolved flames, smoke and nest. Not too many twigs – few and simple are better to be seen at a distance.

▶ A close-up of the head.

◀ Buddha carving in reclaimed English oak.

Meditation

This Westernized version of a seated Buddha was carved without drawings or models showing that sometimes it can be a fun challenge to work in such a spontaneous way.

The Buddha, seated in meditation, is a well-recognized and respected symbol in the West. As a design, the form of the cross-legged meditation pose is a triangle, with the strong base across the knees supporting the body above. This triangular form appears very firm and stable, and gives the Buddha sculpture its solid, calm and somewhat introspective feel – an attractive quality to us more ordinary, volatile human beings.

Buddhism spread and developed into several cultural identities. Thus the treatment of the basic image differs between Japan, Sri Lanka and Tibet. Even though Buddhism arrived in the West many years ago there is, as yet, no comparable Western imagery. No doubt there will be a Western Buddhist sculptural tradition some time in the future, based on the Greek ideals that are at the root of our psyches.

One issue that must be overcome is the Greek ideal of muscular maleness in sculpture, which we still value today. In my opinion, this is inappropriate in a Buddhist context and a bit off-putting to half the population. My version of the image is an attempt to depict the Buddha 'Westernized', rendering the face more androgynous by removing the hard 'male' edge. I also wanted to play down the normally large ears and other imported cultural symbols while still drawing on the traditional iconography of the robe and posture **1** .

1 Detail of the head and face. I am deliberately trying for a Western appearance, halfway between male and female, and to play down the iconography, such as the large ears and 'third eye'.

Strategy

Unusually for me, I made no drawings or models for this carving. I was actually moving the wood from one place to the other and thought: 'I bet if I joined this bit to that, and that to the other, I could carve a Buddha.' I quickly realized I had enough timber to sculpt something reasonably large – the result is 30in (760mm) high – and just started straight in.

Gluing up

The timber came from some lengths of 8 x 3in (200 x 75mm) beams in oak (*Quercus spp.*) that had been well seasoned despite having some quite bad shakes and stains in parts. Unlike many old beams they did not have any nails in them, for which I was eternally grateful.

Because the seated figure was L-shaped when seen from the side, I reckoned I could stack L-shaped blocks together for the centre body and lap, with an extra tall block for the head **2** and **3**, and glue extra pieces to this L-core for thighs and knees. It took a lot of shuffling and measuring to assemble the blocks. In all, I needed 12 pieces. My main concern was to get rid of all the defects within the mass of block, particularly the cracks. The stain was quite widespread and I knew I wouldn't be able to lose it – I would simply have to deal with it by colouring the finished piece in some way, which meant placing the stain in the robes, rather than the body. Lastly, I had to take into account how each piece of wood might move when glued to another and either balance or compensate.

Assembling the pieces to lose the cracks and stains felt somewhere between a crossword puzzle and a jigsaw! At times I certainly didn't feel as calm as the subject I was trying to carve. I ran calculated sections of the beams through a planer to dress them but finished all the joints by hand before gluing them with PVA. I wanted to get the joints as tight as I could. A machine planer leaves an undulating ripple and normally this

2 An L-block – one shoulder and the knees below. You can see the heavy staining and crack which I want to lose by gluing it within the carving.

3 A taller block in the centre for the head. The joints of the two side L-pieces are staggered forward ¼in (6mm) to strengthen the assembly.

2

3

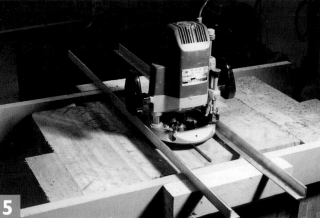

squashes away when the joint is clamped. But with such broad L-faces and hardwood I was going to have to struggle finding enough clamping pressure, so the closer the joint the better.

My way of checking the closeness of joint surfaces is to rub one face with chalk. I offer this to its partner and carefully move it a fraction from side to side. This movement transfers chalk onto any high spots and I selectively skim these down with a plane. I keep doing this until it seems as if no chalk passes from one face to the other. The joint will then be a very tight fit.

Before the glue-up, I create 'keys' by lifting up splinters of wood with a chisel corner all over the joint faces. I started by gluing together my three L-pieces to make the trunk **3** and **4** . Finally, I added side pieces, clamping with everything I had to assemble my starting block.

It had been quite a physical struggle getting this far, working things out on the hoof, but with a block roughly the shape of what I had in mind and the cracks hidden, I began to feel I was getting somewhere. Before I could start sculpting, however, I had one more job to do. As a general rule, I always finish the backs and bases of carvings before I start anything else. It is much harder to work on these areas when the carving is completed. Although my face-to-face joining was good, the underside of the figure wasn't very tidy and it needed to be flattened. It's quite a large area and the best solution seemed to be planing it with a router.

Routing flat surfaces

A lot of people don't know that the router can be used to level and flatten irregular surfaces. It is in fact the ideal tool for very wide boards that won't fit through a planer and those with great big lumps such as mine. The router will perform this particularly useful task very well and quickly, providing you take care to set up accurately.

Essentially you need to make an accurate 'track', along which your router can travel, up and down, skimming the surface of your wood with a wide cutter. In turn, this track must move over the surface you are

4 The completed block with extra pieces for thighs and knees. I've done all this from my head without a drawing, trying to visualize what's inside.

5 Router planing. The router travels up and down the aluminium tacks. These in turn travel from one end of the work to the other along wooden fences. The blocks at the ends of the aluminium tracks act both as spacers and fence guides. You can see how tidy the flattened surface is on the left.

flattening, from end to end. It does this by sitting on two fences **5**. It sounds complicated but is remarkably straightforward to set up. The whole arrangement consists of a jig for guiding the travel of the router over a flat plane. Like all jigs, it is worth taking the trouble to make it accurately and you should be able to reuse it on other projects.

I used two lengths of angle-section aluminium for the 'tracks', but it can be made just as easily from hardwood. The base of the router slides within these angles. Blocks of wood at each end keep the tracks a set distance apart. I wax the metal so the router slides easily. The 'fences' are rails of wood screwed (clamped) to my workpiece, one on either side. Metal strips would also work. The most important thing is that the edges along which the tracks will slide are straight. The fences must be eyed through and exactly parallel or the routed surface will not be flat.

The blocks of wood that hold the tracks apart slide loosely along the outside of the rails. Use a heavy twin-fluted cutter, such as that which might be used for cutting a tenon, of about 1in (25mm) diameter. Don't try to take too big a bite at a time, or one that is too deep. Move the router so the cutter feeds into the work. I skimmed the wood surface by passing the router back and forth, moving incrementally from one end of the block to the other, a bit like ploughing. Lastly, I smoothed over the neatly routed surface with a belt sander. It had taken me about eleven hours of concentrated work to this point and now I could turn to the actual carving.

6 An early stage in the carving where I am trying to find the basic forms within.

7 The texture here shows me swapping from the Arbortech to a large gouge. I placed the cracks and staining to the sides and back, to lose them within the coloured robes.

6

7

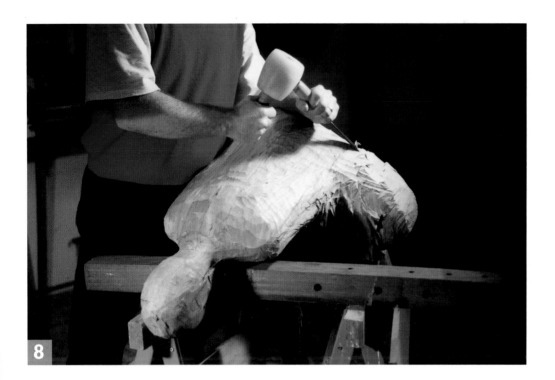

8

The carving

My block was heavy enough to sit on a couple of trestles for carving. Without drawings or a model, I had to work my imagination overtime, strongly visualizing the form beneath. There are ways of starting the journey into the desert of blank canvas of which the first and perhaps the best is to decide on points where you definitely *don't* want to take wood away. These will be your high spots, and it's downhill from here 6.

In this case, I marked points at the shoulders, sternum, knees, elbows and nose as principal landmarks. The work followed the normal process of roughing out and bosting, through to the modelling and final details. I used an Arbortech and large gouges for the initial roughing out, passing back and forth between the two 7 and 8.

The final wood surface ended quite smooth with flat gouges and I normally leave my carvings finished at this stage. However, in this case I wanted to try and get an even smoother surface. I removed all gouge marks first with rasps. I use hand-cut rasps, as made by Auriou, which are more expensive than machine-cut rasps but give a much smoother finish. From fine rasping I passed easily onto scraping. I make my scrapers from old files, ground to a sharp edge. I find I can get very near to a finished surface and only need a little sanding to complete the job.

Hollowing out

With so many different pieces of wood in my block, newly carved, I felt that there might be a 'settling down' – an adjustment of shapes and thus pressures – that might cause either cracking or the joints to open up. To minimize this possibility I hollowed the figure out from below as best I could. As all woodturners know a 'hollow form' will move and alter shape with less likelihood of cracking than a solid one.

Hollowing was a taxing job entailing an Arbortech, bent gouges and a flexible shaft with a Rod Naylor Tornado cutter. Had I thought through this project beforehand instead of tearing straight into it, I would have created this internal space when I glued-up.

Finishing

The 'natural', and unwanted, stains in oak are dark blue. The real problem for me was that any joint where one board was stained and the next one wasn't, showed very clearly and obtrusively. I really don't mind joins in carvings but I would rather they remain in the background. I had kept the staining away from the skin but it was very obvious among the robes.

I used a two-part bleach to remove the blue stains but of course the resulting patches of white were just as bad. I needed some colour that would merge these bleached patches with the rest of the wood and in a serendipitous moment I realised the solution was in my hand even as I contemplated the problem – coffee.

I made up a weak solution of powdered coffee, experimented, made up stronger, played around a bit more, and eventually managed to get the bleached stains somewhere near an oak colour. I then washed all the robes and hair with coffee to unify, and consolidated the new stains with Danish oil. You can still see a difference in colour across some of the joins but the level is acceptable and not too noticeable.

I gave the whole figure, including the naked wood of the skin, a final coat of beeswax. It was not so much the carving but the wood that dominated this project – from blocking up to hollowing out, and removing stains. And in there was the ideal I was trying to carve. I think that if I had planned the carving, with drawings and perhaps a clay model, I could have saved myself a lot of time. Had I done so it would neither have been as challenging nor as fun.

NUMBER

Straight tools	Long-bent tools	Short-bent tools	Back-bent tools	2 ¹⁄₁₆	3 ⅛	5 ³⁄₁₆	6 ¼	8 ⁵⁄₁₆	10 ⅜	11 ⁷⁄₁₆	13 ½	14 ⁹⁄₁₆	16 ⅝	20 ¾	22 ⅞
1	–	21	–												
2	–	22–3	–												
3	12	24	33												
4	13	25	34												
5	14	26	35												
6	15	27	36												
7	16	28	37												
8	17	29	38												
9	18	30	–												
10	19	31	–												
11	20	32	–												
39	40	43	–												
41	42	44	–												
45	46	–	–												

TTING EDGE

26	30	32	36	38	mm
1	1⅛	1¼	1⅜	1½	ins

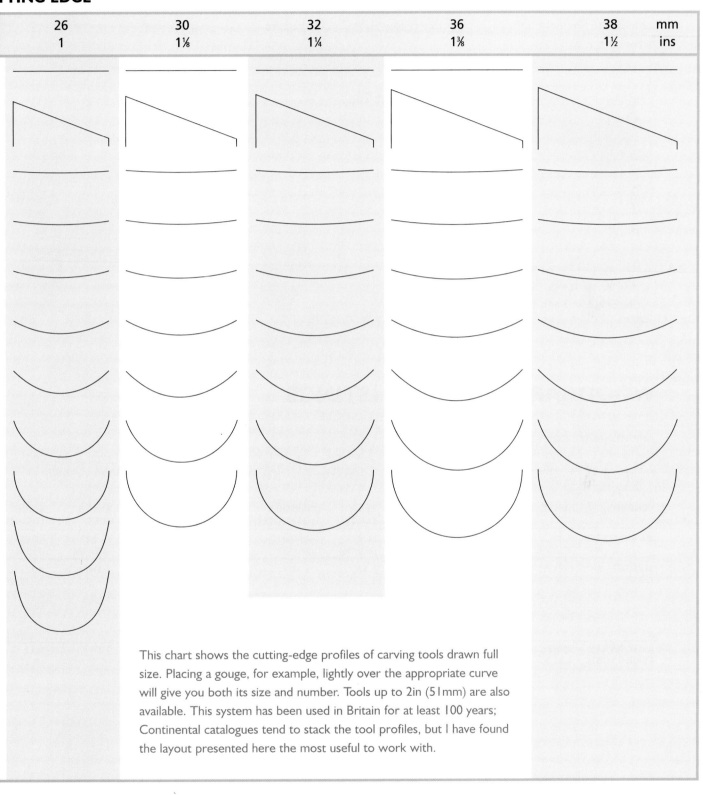

This chart shows the cutting-edge profiles of carving tools drawn full size. Placing a gouge, for example, lightly over the appropriate curve will give you both its size and number. Tools up to 2in (51mm) are also available. This system has been used in Britain for at least 100 years; Continental catalogues tend to stack the tool profiles, but I have found the layout presented here the most useful to work with.

The Pfeil System

Pfeil uses a different numbering system to the Sheffield list, although the actual shapes are the same. For example a Pfeil number 2 gouge is the same as the Sheffield number 3. The table below shows a comparison between the two.

Pfeil Cut	Sheffield List No. Sweep
2	3
3	slightly quicker 4
5	5
7	6
8	slightly flatter 8
9	9
11	11
39 (60° V tool)	12

Sheffield List 7 and 10 are missing

WOODCARVING TOOL LISTINGS

APPROXIMATE CONVERSIONS

¹⁄₁₆in=1.5mm	³⁄₃₂in=2.25mm	⅛in=3mm	³⁄₁₆in=4.5mm	¼in=6mm	⁵⁄₁₆in=7.5mm	⅜in=9mm	⁷⁄₁₆in=10.5mm	½in=12mm
⅝in=15mm	¾in=19mm	⅞in=22mm	1in=25mm	1¼in=32mm	1½in=37mm	2in=50mm	2⅜in=60mm	3in=70mm

COMPANY	ASHLEY ILES	AURIO (CLASSICHT)	FLEX-CUT (BRIMARC)	HENRY TAYLOR	KIRSCHEN (AXMINSTER)	MHG (RUTLANDS)	PFEIL (TILGEAR)	ROBERT SORBY	STUBAI (TIRANTI)
MANUFACTURED	UK (IMP.) SWEEP/INCH	FRANCE SWEEP/MM	US (IMP.) SWEEP/INCH	UK (IMP.) SWEEP/INCH	GERMANY SWEEP/MM	GERMANY SWEEP/MM	SWITZERLAND SWEEP/MM	UK (IMP.) SWEEP/INCH	AUSTRIA SWEEP/MM
STRAIGHT CHISEL	1 SWP: ¹⁄₁₆, ³⁄₃₂, ⅛, ³⁄₁₆, ¼, ⁵⁄₁₆, ⅜, ⁷⁄₁₆, ½, ⅝, ¾, ⅞, 1, 1¼, 1½, 2, 2⅜, 3in	1 SWP: 10, 12, 14, 15, 16, 18, 20, 22, 25, 30, 40	MALLET TOOLS 1 SWP: ½, ¾, 1, 1¼in HAND TOOLS ⅜, ⅝, ⅞in	1 SWP: ⅜, ¼, ½, ¾, 1in	1 SWP: 3, 6, 10, 16	4, 6, 10, 16	1 SWP: 3, 6, 10, 16 1, 1/E SWP: 2, 3, 5, 8, 12, 16, 20, 25, 30, 35	1 SWP: ⅜in	NO.1: 2, 4, 6, 10, 12, 16, 20, 25, 30, 40, 50
SKEW CHISEL/ CORNER CHISEL	2 SWP: ¹⁄₁₆, ³⁄₃₂, ⅛, ³⁄₁₆, ¼, ⁵⁄₁₆, ⅜, ⁷⁄₁₆, ½, ⅝, ¾, ⅞, 1, 1¼, 1½, 2, 2⅜, 3in	1 SWP: 1, 2, 3, 4, 5, 6, 8, 10, 12, 14, 15, 16, 18, 20, 22, 25, 30, 40	MALLET TOOLS 2 SWP: ½, ¾, ¹⁵⁄₁₆, 1³⁄₁₆in	1 SWP: ⁵⁄₁₆, ⅜, ⅝in NO.22 / 1 SWP: ⅛in NO.23 / 1 SWP: ⅛in	2 SWP: 6, 10, 19	6, 10, 18	1/S, 1/SE SWP: 2, 3, 5, 8, 12, 16, 20, 25, 30, 35	2 SWP: ⅛, ⅜in	NO.2: 2, 4, 6, 10, 12, 16, 2, 25,

Glossary

A

alongee a carving tool splaying directly from the shoulder.

B

background the plane against which the whole subject is placed. See gound.

bell flower usually as a drop, small ornamental, bell-shaped flowers.

bent carving tools have a curve or crank along their length. This allows them to get deeper into recesses without catching the wood around the edge and juddering. Always push the tool forwards to cut; never lever. Longbent (salmon, sowback, curved) gouges are bent along the whole blade length for shallower recesses. Shortbent (spoon, spoonbit) tools have a long shank with a (to a greater or lesser degree) tight crank at the blade, for getting in deeper hollows. Backbent tools are reversed shortbents for use when the tool is to be presented to the wood when you want to carve into a hollow with the gouge in an 'upside down' (cannel to wood) position.

bevel the wedge of metal between the cutting edge and the heel. There may be bevel on outside or the inside. Outer bevels should be kept as flat as possible for most use; and stropped to a polish, so sliding more easily through the wood.
A correct cutting angle is important. Inner bevels are never found on gouges bought straight from the manufacturer, leading the inexperienced to think is the norm. However an inside bevel of even 5° has enormous benefits – particularly when a gouge is used 'upside down'.

bosting or 'bosting in' is the very important stage after crude roughing out when the principal forms are positioned and the flow of the carving is sketched in. It underpins all subsequent shaping and modelling.

C

cannel (sounding like 'camel', not 'canal') refers to the inside face of any carving tool: deep or flat gouge, V tool etc. Usually 'in cannel' to differentiate from 'out cannel', the opposite, outer face.

curved gouges see bent tools.

cusp the small triangular point between the foils in gothic tracery. The cusps may have a triangular, inverted pyramid carved into them.

cutting there are many ways of manipulating and making cuts with carving tools and all carvers need as much versatility as possible here. Key terms are:
Running cut a long cut with V tools, fluters or deep gouges; as in lining in or decorating the wood surface.
Slicing cut the gouge is given a sideways movement as it is pushed forwards. This may involve simply 'drifting' to the side - sometimes called 'sliding' - or rotating the handle a little, or both. The cutting edge may be sliced to the left or the right and is particularly seen with flatter gouges and vital for dealing with instances of awkward grain.
Sweep cut or sweeping cut a slice cut with emphasis on rotating the gouge by the handle along the sweep. It is particularly seen in deeper gouges which can make full use of their perfectly shaped sweeps to set in clean outlines.
Rocking or rocking cuts are just short sweep cuts. The principal way of carving wood. The handle is given a quick twist (rotated) as it is moved forward, slicing out chip. This is much cleaner cutting than simple pushing the tool along straight.
Stop cut a short stab cut which limits the extent to which wood fibres may tear.
Stab cut pushing the cutting edge straight in and out of the wood either for decorative purposes or as a stop cut.

cutting angle is the angle between the bevel and the surface of the wood – it can only be measured if both faces are flat. Find it by placing the carving tool on the bench; slide it forward as you raise the handle and the tool 'bites' the wood at the cutting angle. 15–20° is fine for the majority of medium-density carving woods. Rounded bevels raise the cutting angle and so decrease tool control; and increase the size of the bevel 'wedge'.

cutting edge invisible to the naked eye and must be very sharp – with its corners. Remember that you can have a very sharp cutting edge but a carving tool which cuts poorly if the bevel is incorrectly shaped or at the wrong cutting angle.

D

detailing the final stage when all the surface decoration is carved. A very common mistake is for beginners to put in details too early – when they end up in the wrong place and fix the carving to early. They do it because they are thinking 'surface' and feel safe with something 'caught'. However details are never the problem. If the underlying forms are correctly bosted and modelled, trust that details will just fall into place.

E

edge the hard end of a plane. Its strength depends on the lie of the grain and the degree of undercutting. Differentiate from a form horizon.

F

facets small planes or divots remaining after the cutting edge has passed – what they look like depends on the quickness of the gouge and how the tool was handled. They can be made purposeful – adding 'meaning' to the work or surface – or simply ways of texturing.

finishing may mean either 'finishing off' a carving: the last carving (detailing or 'licking up') stages; or colouring, sealing or waxing the finished piece.

fishtails gouges or chisels which splay suddenly at the cutting end from a long shank. Lightweight with an emphasis on the corners for finer finishing work. Easily overheat with grinding.

flat gouges see sweep.

flute a long deep channel with circular root. Fluting is the arranging of such flutes in rows in, for example, furniture legs etc.

fluter a deep U-shaped gouge, used for running deep channels Importantly, it is used in a different manner to arc-based gouges – because of its straight sides – hence its name: it is more than just a deep gouge.

foil the lobe effect formed by the inner curves or arcs of gothic tracery; each foil ends at the cusp.

form a rather loose term meaning the external shape of something, the disposition of masses of parts. Not the colour, subject-matter or surface, but more how the object is occupying space. See shape.

form horizon my own term for the apparent line where the surface of a soft form (such as a hill or ball) disappears from view. Distinguish this from a simple, hard edge. A form horizon seems fixed when drawn on paper as a line (an outline), but in reality there is no such line, only a horizon which changes with the viewpoint. Fixed, hard edges (such as a wing or fishtail) remain relatively stable as the viewpoint changes. Why is this idea important? When moving from a two-dimensional drawing to a three-dimensional relief carving, you must know what your lines really represent, and how the result may be viewpoint dependent.

froster A punch that has cross-hatched teeth (rather like a miniature meat tenderizer or stone carver's bouchard) for texturing a surface with tiny points. Also called a 'matting tool'.

G

glyptic from the Greek 'to carve': sculpture or other work formed by carving or reductive methods. Such work should clearly differentiate from plastic or modelled processes.

ground any plane in front of which another plane (or part of the carving) is raised. So, say you are wearing a shirt; your wrist then becomes the 'ground' for the cuff; the cuff would be the 'ground' for the button and so on. Differentiate this from background.

grounding out or, **gronding** is the process whereby a ground or background is reduced to a specified level. It usually involves a rapid lowering stage followed by levelling to finish off the surface.

grounding tool or grounder a shortbent flat carving tool for finishing enclosed grounds. In the past flat chisels were often used, at a time when a lot of grounds with low relief furniture carving were punched or matted over. The torn grain left by the digging in of chisel corners could be disguised. Today the tool of choice is more likely a No 3 (flattest) gouge which will leave a very smooth flat ground while keeping corners clear.

H

heel the ridge where bevel meets blade proper. Smooth it over to make sure it burnishes the wood after the cutting edge, and does not scratch it.

high relief a loose term, as is low relief, without a numerical value: the background in such carving is relatively deep compared with the width of the subject. It would be fair to say a background depth of about a quarter of the subject's width is high relief. As high relief gets deeper so the subject approaches full three dimensions.

I, J

incising literally 'cutting': any surface carving with gouge, V tool etc. If a carving is just incised, it would not have involved grounding out.

intaglio (pron. without the 'g'. Syn: diaglyph) literally to 'engrave' a surface. The subject is incised but the background is left untouched. A buttermould and many Egyptian wall reliefs would be examples of intaglio carving.

junction the line where a wall meets the ground. Always leave junctions clean and neat, even when deeply undercut. Poor toolwork here shows a lack of professionalism and a sign of incompetence.

L

levelling finishing off a background to a smooth plane; its success depends on a careful lowering, waste removal, beforehand. A background need only appear flat and level, it is not necessary to be precise like an engineer.

licking up a trade term for a final going over and tidying of a carving.

lining in outlining a subject in relief carving – quickly and approximately – with V tool or fluter to protect it when the surrounding waste wood is removed. Also allows safe setting in, without danger of the wedge-like action of the bevel weakening or breaking wood fibres.

lowering removing waste from a ground or background to a required level. It is worth doing this methodically and precisely – the final levelling finish is then very quick and exact.

low relief a shallow, but arbitrary, depth of carving. As with high relief it is not so much the actual physical depth of the background as the relationship of this depth to the subject. A background at, say, a 30th of the subject width would definitely be low relief. A huge Assyrian lion wall relief may be many, many times deeper in actual inches but still be classed as a similar level of low relief because the ratio of depth of background to subject is the same.

M

mass is contrasted with space, both of which are present and sensed in a carving and must be considered of equal importance in a design. Carvers create space by removing the mass, but paradoxically it is space they work with. Mass appears to arise in the carving as the space is removed, even though it was all there in the original block.

matting tool see froster.

modelling a stage after the principle underlying forms (see bosting) have been established. Secondary and further forms are carved, gradually refining the carving and leading on to final detailing.

O, P

outlining a good alternative word to lining in, although 'the outline' is usually taken to be the principal one surrounding the whole subject, with a background, whereas lining in can refer to separating any subject from its ground.

parting tool alternative name for a V tool, which points to a key V tool function: separating one part from another.

pierced relief carving the background is completely cut away or in parts. Remember that whatever is seen through the piercings, wallpaper even, will become a part of the carving.

plane implies a two-dimensional surface. In woodcarving generally (including sculpture) parts with a flat (or flattish) surface; it is in the nature of cutting with chisels and gouges to emphasis changes of plane, distinguishing glyptic from plastic work. In relief carving one can use 'plane' simply to mean a different level, as in a 'change of plane' (change of level) which may not be truly flat.

plastic from the greek 'to mould': sculpture or other work formed in soft material such as clay by modelling or additive methods. Such work should clearly differentiate from glyptic or carved processes.

punches small bars of metal with shaped ends for indenting, either for cleaning and levelling the bottom of a small hole for example, or for decorating a surface. See froster.

Q, R

quercus species of oak.

quick gouges a gouge is said to be getting 'quicker' as it gets deeper in cross-section.

relief carving lies in its own world, somewhere between painting and sculpture, with the depth dimension diminished and subjects usually related to a virtual, original, surface plane and set against a background plane. See low and high relief carving.

S

sculpture a loose term of wide interpretation for three-dimensional work. I use it to mean carvings which are fully three-dimensional: 'in-the-round'; as compared with a relief carving where the depth dimension is less than in reality. There are two important approaches to creating in three dimensions and it is very important for carvers to understand and appreciate the difference: glyptic and plastic.

setting in the precise shaping of an outline around a subject by matching sweeps to curves or slicing the line with the cutting edge.

shank the varying length or square metal between the shoulder (or handle if no shoulder present) and the blade of a carving tool.

shape sometimes used as an alternative to form. I tend to use the term as an aspect of form, to mean the configuration of an edge or area, how the surface of the three-dimensional object appears. So shape is something more that two-dimensional even if actually moving through space.

shoulder a flange which prevents the carving tool from being driven into the handle and splitting it proper. Also called 'bolster' or 'stop'.

slip/slipstone small shaped stones for working the inside of gouges or V tools.

spade tools splay out along their length. Roughly depending on the ratio between shank and blade you get fishtail, allongee and spade tools. Spades are somewhere betwen the two with roughly equal amounts of shank to blade. They are also called 'pod' or 'long pod' tools.

surface this is always what you actually see – it is a mistake, and a lost opportunity, not to make full use of it and the qualities you can give it as a carver.

sweep the curvature of a gouge in cross-section, being an arc of a circle. Gouges are identified by how much curve there is, from 'flat' (almost, but definitely not, a chisel) to 'deep' (or 'quick', the quickest being a semicircle), with 'medium' in between.

T

tang the sharp end of a carving tool which fits into, and should be in line with, the handle.

tracery loose term (deriving from Sir Christopher Wren and not found in medieval contracts) for the repeating, lace-like patterns of lines, bars and lobe-like decoration found in gothic architecture furniture. More delicacy is achievable by woodcarvers because wooden tracery is non-weight bearing, unlike stone. May be pierced or panelled. Usually laid out geometrically although the oldest are done purely by eye.

U, V

undercutting also known as backing off, cutting an edge or form horizon from behind to increase the sense of thinness or relief.

veiner a small (⅛in, 3mm or less) deep gouge, or U-shaped gouge. See fluter.

V tool a very important tool in the carver's repertoire consisting of two chisels meeting at an angle of 60° (commonest), 90° or 45°. The line along which they meet is known as the keel. Used in particular for lining in and creating decorative grooves. Also known as a parting tool.

W

wall the side plane of a subject, having depth and to which a ground junction is made. It may also have a surface edge. The term may also describe the side walls of an incised letter.

wasting removing unwanted wood so as to approach the surface form or outline of a subject.

Z

zoomorphics designs or ornamentation based on the forms of animals, birds, fish etc. Particularly important in European Celtic art where they first started making an appearance in the Bronze Age.

Tool suppliers UK

Alec Tiranti Ltd
Mail order and showroom:
3 Pipers Court
Berkshire Drive
Thatcham
Berkshire
RG19 4ER
tel: +44 (0) 845 1232100
www.tiranti.co.uk

Shop also at:
27 Warren Street
London
W1T 5NB
tel: +44 (0) 20 76368565

Ashley Iles (Edge Tools) Ltd
East Kirkby
Spilsby
Lincolnshire
PE23 4DD
tel: +44 (0) 1790 763372
www.ashleyiles.turningtools.co.uk

Classic Hand Tools
77 High Street
Needham Market
Suffolk
IP6 8AN
tel: +44 (0) 1449 721327
www.classichandtools.com

Craft Supplies
The Mill
Millers Dale
Buxton
SK17 8SN
tel: +44 (0) 1433 622550
www.craft-supplies.co.uk

Henry Taylor Tools Ltd
The Forge
Peacock Estate
Livesey Street
Sheffield
S6 2BL
tel: +44 (0) 1142 340282
www.henrytaylortools.co.uk

**John Boddy's Fine Wood
& Tool Store Ltd**
Riverside Sawmills
Boroughbridge
North Yorkshire
YO51 9LJ
tel: +44 (0) 1423 322370
www.john-boddys-fwts.co.uk

Tilgear
Bridge House
69 Station Road
Cuffley
Potters Bar
Hertfordshire
EN6 4TG
tel: +44 (0) 1707 873434

Tool suppliers USA

Tools for Working Wood
27 West 20th Street
Suite 507
New York
NY 10011
www.toolsforworkingwood.com

Wood Carvers Supply Inc
PO Box 7500
Englewood
FL 34295-7500
tel: +1 941 698 0123
www.woodcarverssupply.com

Woodcraft
210 Wood County Industrial Park
PO Box 1686
Parkersburg
WV 26102
tel: +1 800 225 1153
www.woodcraft.com

Recommended Reading

Denning, Anthony *The Craft of Woodcarving* (Cassell, 1994)

Hasluck, Paul *Manual of Traditional Woodcarving* (Dover, 1978)

MacTaggart, Peter and Ann *Practical Gilding* (Mac & Me Ltd, 1984)

Norbury, Ian *Relief Woodcarving and Lettering* (Stobart, 1987)

Norbury, Ian *Carving Classic Female Figures in Wood* (Fox Chapel, 2004)

Norbury, Ian *Carving Classic Female Faces in Wood* (Fox Chapel, 2004)

Onians, Dick *Essential Woodcarving Techniques* (GMC Publications, 1997)

Pye, Chris *Woodcarving Tools, Materials & Equipment* (GMC Publications, 1994)

Pye, Chris *Carving on Turning* (GMC Publications, 1995)

Pye, Chris *Lettercarving in Wood* (GMC Publications, 1997)

Pye, Chris *Relief Carving in Wood* (GMC Publications, 1998)

Pye, Chris *Elements of Woodcarving* (GMC Publications, 2000)

Pye, Chris *Woodcarving Tools, Materials & Equipment, New Edition, Volume I* (GMC Publications, 2002)

Pye, Chris *Woodcarving Tools, Materials & Equipment New Edition, Volume II* (GMC Publications, 2002)

Schnute, William J *High Relief Woodcarving* (Sterling, 1985)

Wheeler, William and Hayward, Charles *Practical Woodcarving and Gilding* (Evans, 1983)

Wilbur, Frederick *Carving Architectural Detail in Wood* (GMC Publications, 2000)

About the Author

CHRIS PYE has been woodcarving since 1975 and is a member of the Master Carvers Association. His work is eclectic and ranges from architectural and figure carving to lettering and furniture – such as bedheads and fireplaces. Clients include HRH the Prince of Wales.

A well-respected woodcarving teacher, Chris specializes in one-to-one personal woodcarving tuition and has taught classes regularly in the USA for over ten years. He has written extensively on woodcarving for magazines and his previous books for GMC Publications are: *Woodcarving Tools, Materials & Equipment, Carving on Turning, Lettercarving in Wood, Relief Carving in Wood, Elements of Woodcarving, Woodcarving Tools, Materials & Equipment, New Edition* (revised and expanded in two volumes).

www.chrispye-woodcarving.com is dedicated to the teaching, learning and love of woodcarving.

Index

Contact us for a complete catalogue, or visit our website.
GMC Publications Ltd, 166 High Street, Lewes, East Sussex BN7 1XU, United Kingdom
Tel: 01273 488005 Fax: 01273 402866
www.gmcbooks.com